Liberal vs. Conservative: The Coming Civil War

Timothy Lawton

ISBN: 1-4392-0266-4
ISBN-13: 9781439202661

Visit www.booksurge.com to order additional copies.

CONTENTS

FOREWORD

This book is merely a glancing look at the issues we face in our day. Almost every chapter could be made into a book on its own. My purpose here is not to solve all of the issues that face us. To the contrary I am hoping to show how the disparate means that liberals and conservatives use to address the problems we face in our society are no longer able to be compromised. Yes, there are still areas in which the two can find commonality, but they are fading quickly. Years ago the foundations upon which both the right and the left existed were essentially the same; they may have had differing ideas on policy, but the overall basis for their beliefs was founded on the same fundamental principles. I feel that it is safe to say that this is no longer the case.

I would love to have a concrete suggestion for every path we should take, but I don't. It is my goal to use the grey matter between my ears to the best of the abilities that God has given me. Where I do make specific suggestions I stand by them. Where I cannot I hope that the minds of others may be sparked to investigate the problems I try to address in these pages. Many of the issues of our time are fraught with extreme complexities. Experts in many fields are needed to research the varied solutions to the problems that plague our nation and world. Yet, it must be understood that common ground will be hard to find between the differing viewpoints that have evolved into what we see in the twenty-first century.

It is my purpose to make this book as readable as possible. I will try to include facts and figures only when necessary. In many cases I use my own insights and experiences to explain why I believe what I believe. These pages contain the best thoughts that I was able to produce in late 2007 and early 2008. America and the world are at the beginning of one of the greatest crises faced by mankind. It is not a single threat like the Black Plague, but a myriad of challenges that face us on every side. It seems that the world is about ready to tumble like a house of cards. From the environment to culture, from politics to natural disasters, the headlines we read are certainly interesting. Yet, I recall a Chinese proverb which states, May you live in interesting times. Though it may seem like a compliment it is actually an insult. Think of it: When is mankind at his most interesting? When we stand at the gates of our most intense misfortune. Sadly, I think we stand before those gates today. May God have mercy on our souls!

LIBERAL VS. CONSERVATIVE: THE COMING CIVIL WAR

Some may think that the title of this book is facetious, or an attempt to garner attention. Sadly, I cannot claim those innocuous reasons for the title. In truth, I believe that the differences between these two polar viewpoints will eventually lead to the disintegration of America as we know it, and the downfall of Western civilization as a whole. It may take decades, even centuries, but this clash of ideals is inevitable. Like the certainty of an incoming tide this battle has been creeping up on us for quite some time, from the dawn of the Enlightenment to our present day. Each ideology has had its time and place, but the crossroads of their incompatibility is approaching rapidly.

My hope is not to write a prophecy of doom, but to extol the virtue of truth into this debate. I will not hide my partisanship: I consider myself a conservative. Yet that does not mean that I don't have a respect for both points of view. Liberals have brought a great deal of benefit to our culture, especially in the realms of tolerance and freedom. Conservatives have kept the instruments that have preserved the institutions necessary to allow society to function. Both systems of thought have made our society what it is today. Both groups have offered something that has helped to make us great, but in their purest sense their mutual benefit is no longer viable. The time has come when their compatibility is no longer acceptable to either of the two ideologies. America, the Western world, must go one way or the other.

Recent decades have exacerbated the chasm that exists between the liberal and the conservative. Issues of life and death, technology, religion, science, government programs, economy, social interaction, family, global affairs, and a host of other issues have clearly delineated the significant differences that exist between them. The approaches to tackling these problems, and opportunities, grow ever more diverse with each passing day. Virtually every major issue of our time sees these two factions attempting to address the issue in completely different manners.

The current political climate of the world exemplifies the disparity between liberals and conservatives as never before. Both foreign and domestic policy issues delineate the opposing viewpoints by which we approach the world. Liberals look to engage, negotiate, and compromise. Conservatives hope to act, pressure, and exemplify. Yet, the former fail to appreciate the disparities that exist between Western culture and much of the rest of the world. They project their belief systems onto other peoples in the world without realizing that they do not see the world through Judeo-Christian eyes.

Yes, I just associated the West with Judeo-Christianity. And this does include most of you wide-eyed atheists, agnostics, and pagans. The belief that love is the ultimate power in the universe is Judeo-Christian. Whether the left likes it or not our most cherished beliefs are biblical. "Love your neighbor as yourself, love your enemies, pray for those who persecute you." These are Judeo-Christian values and history is indebted to the likes of Abraham, Moses, Isaiah, Jesus, Peter, and Paul. To fail to understand this point is to misunderstand the culture of the West.

Yet, this is the exact reason that the policies of the liberals in dealing with other cultures are failing worldwide. This misunderstanding of the left is exemplified in their inability to understand the nature of the jihad being waged against us to their unwillingness to see illegal immigration as the threat it actually poses. We are as Rome. We are rotting from within and allowing outside forces to pervert our culture. Don't get me wrong: I do associate Rome with the worst excesses that our culture has ever endured, but the analogy is quite apt. We weaken ourselves with pleasure and indulgence, while our barbarians blow themselves up in the street and others create vast global empires which bide their time until we are weak enough to attack.

The time of the liberal is done. They take the best of Jesus and turn it over on its head. Jesus never said, "Turn the other cheek again, and again, and again until you're bludgeoned to death!" He was wise enough to ask us to do it only once. "There is a time for peace and a time for war." Since 9/11 I have realized that this is war. The time to negotiate and understand has long passed. Communists, fascists and jihadists do not see the inherent worth and value of each and every man. They do not see the inalienable rights of life, liberty, and the pursuit of happiness. Trust me, I hate war. I despise it, I have studied it all too much and for far too long, but if you never feel you need to fight then you are at the mercy of those who will.

On domestic issues the chasm is no less wide. America has illegal immigrants openly protesting in our streets with impunity and columns of self-professed humanitarians marching in Washington, D.C., demanding their right to decide who will live and who will die. Liberals want to redistribute the wealth of the nation through government decree. They want to give constitutional rights to terrorists and to those who flagrantly violated our laws and are here illegally. Eminent domain is used to steal our property and our Constitution is viewed as a fluid document ready to be changed at the whim of a judge.

The times are dire. Yet, few seem to see the inevitable march of this madness if it is left unchecked. When will we realize that our rights are disappearing and sanity is no longer part of our society? The battle between liberal and conservative is no longer a political parlor game. It is a serious war that will decide how, and what, our culture does to address the incredible challenges that face us in the present and future.

What we choose today can very well mean the existence or extinction of the human race.

In the following pages I hope to examine the many issues facing our nation and world. My goal is to suggest the possible solutions to these problems. I also intend to show how the incompatibility of liberalism and conservatism makes it virtually impossible for these two viewpoints to compromise any further on just about all the challenges society faces. I believe that it is primarily the left that is causing this war within our culture. It is not enough for them to live and let live, but they feel it necessary to impose their beliefs onto the community at large. This is particularly evident in public education, religion in the public domain, and the debate about same sex marriage.

Our democracy cannot survive in homogenous groups separated from one another. Yet, the reconciliation of vastly different world views is extremely unlikely. This problem is also exacerbated by the use of judicial fiat to alter our Constitution and arbitrarily change laws. The use of the courts to pursue political enemies has been employed by all sides. Look at debates and we see the unwillingness of either side to even agree on what the facts are that form the basis on which to have a discussion. Finally, we see the extreme points of view from the radical left, which blames America for all the problems of the world, even going as far as saying that we attacked ourselves on 9/11.

I can live with people in our democracy if they respect our Constitution, but it becomes impossible when they try to impose their world view on every aspect of society. When the family, religion, and personal liberty are subject to constant attack, at what point am I no longer free to pursue what makes me happy? When all morality is viewed as subjective there is no basis for community. When commonsense is attacked and accommodation made for every minority point of view, no matter how extreme, society no longer has a foundation to exist upon. Absolute democracy is as damning as absolute power!

CIVIL RIGHTS, RACISM, AND PREJUDICE

Being a history teacher, this is a subject I get to deal with very often, from the horrors of our past to the fact that our nation has come so far when it comes to equality. Yet, this is an issue on which I greatly disagree with the liberals. The only thing they do with these topics is divide people into separate groups, make America look worse than it is, and blame all problems on the white man. History is a lot more complex than that, and race relations are one of the most misunderstood areas in this discipline. There is no question that prejudice and racism have played a significant role in American and world history. There is also no question that the benefits of this have primarily been to white men, and that blacks, women, Indians, and other minority groups have suffered the most. Yet, the idea that this simple paradigm didn't have more eclectic nuances to it is simply ignorance.

I hate politically correct terminology and I refuse to use it. I call people what they are. I also can prove that those politically correct terms are incapable of having the meaning ascribed to them. When one says African-American, what is truly meant? Is that person speaking of the Arab Egyptian? Is he speaking of the sephardic Jews who have lived in North Africa for centuries, or talking about black people indigenous from the central Sahara to Capetown in the south of the African continent. Is a white Russian from Vladivostok an Asian-American?

Let me cite a specific example. Several years ago I had a student from Israel. He was born and raised in the country until he came to the U.S. Yet, his family originally came from Morocco. The religion of his family was Jewish. So I ask you, liberals, which label should this young man be given under your politically correct code? Should he be an Asian-American, an African-American, or Jewish-American? The only one of those labels that would match what you intend in your terminology would be Jewish-American, yet he could justifiably be called any of them. He and I used to joke about having him apply to colleges using the exact same applications, but changing the ethnic designations on each one. Our hope was to see how the ethnicity change altered his acceptance to colleges. Too bad we never got to try out this plan because he got kicked out of my school. Oddly enough, this student was able to pass himself off as white, Latino, Italian, and, of course, Israeli. Hopefully I have sufficed to make my point on politically correct terminology.

As I'm attempting to write this chapter I realize I'm going to have a hard time not having this turn into a history lesson. Who knows, maybe that might be the best way to convey my ideas on this topic. The first thing that we must consider when we discuss these issues is the spirit of America. In my classes I teach that the spirit of America is the Declaration of Independence, and that the law of the land is the federal Constitution. When we look to the Declaration we see the phrase "All men are created equal." We know that this has not always been the case, nor is it the case even today, but we can easily ascertain that we have made steady progress on this ideal. When our nation was first established, only a fraction of the adult populace was allowed to vote; the only exception that I know of which still exists is that some states prohibit convicted felons from voting after they have served their time. This is a true salute to our ability to eventually meet the lofty goals set out by our founders.

Understandably, racism and prejudice can be very touchy issues. Frequently I find myself walking a tightrope in the classroom, and in personal discussions, trying not to have the sensibilities of any participant in a debate be offended. Yet, at some point we just have to take our chances and speak what we mean. Sometimes I feel as if those on the left are almost looking to find some reason to become indignant. They want to be offended so they can cast aspersions on those who do not see things in quite the same way they do. This does nothing but promote animosity and further separate us as people. If we are ever going to mitigate prejudice to the insignificant place where it belongs we need to recognize the personal perceptions that we all hold as individuals. This issue can not be discussed unless we can understand the different ways in which race, nationality, sex, and religion help each person form the foundation of how they view their place in the world.

There is no question that racism and prejudice still play a role in the daily lives of the American people. Yet, we have to look at what still remains to be done on the legal front, and what must be done by individuals in their interpersonal relationships. For all intents and purposes racism and prejudice are effectively outlawed in this nation. Now, that does not mean that it plays no role in the life of our society. On the contrary, these prejudices still exist in the hearts and minds of many people. Oftentimes it is a factor that determines with whom one will associate, who one will hire, who one will admit into an organization, and who will enter a school of higher education. To this day I still feel that it is minority groups that are affected the most adversely, but since the Civil Rights Act of 1964 much has improved in the integration of our society. The question now becomes how will we continue to make race, sex, religion, and ethnicity least affect the opportunities that individuals have presented to them. It may sound obvious but some segregation, such as male and female bathroom facilities, are still desirable. Absolute equality can become just as oppressive as inequality. Equality means that we are equal under the law and opportunity according to the gifts God has given each of us.

I feel that the law has done just about all that it can do on this front. In fact, some of the places where race, sex, and ethnicity help one achieve their goals should be reconsidered. Diversity is good so long as it does not inhibit the best from entering jobs or institutions. How many would want to see affirmative action applied to professional sports? At what point do the special considerations given to minorities in order to help them catch up in society become a crutch? At what point does singling out minority groups for special treatment become a point of contention among the varying groups in this country? When does true freedom mean allowing people to simply sink or swim becomes the basis for our society? I'm not saying to eliminate all considerations of minority status, but I am saying we need to start to wean ourselves from such methods. Maintaining race, sex, and ethnicity as a focus only serves to divide us more deeply into our respective groups.

Often we see people trying to change the language we use in society. Usually it is a ridiculous concept based on poor liberal reasoning. My favorite example of this is the feminist use of the term herstory. As if history was supposed to be "his story." The word history only accidentally has that chance spelling in English. This pitiful attempt to imply some sort of elitism on the part of men is patently absurd. Anyway, how will this new word change society? By the empowerment of women who otherwise would not have succeeded in life had they attended world history class instead of world herstory class? If one's self view is tied to something so minute then you probably would not succeed anyway. Changing our terminology in such manners is only a sign of a weak intellectual position.

I have encountered similar situations in other cases. One was when I was attending college in the mid-1990s. I forget what class it was in, but a debate broke out about the figurative uses of the words white and black. I remember my astonishment when students started to say that the association of black with bad and white with good somehow affected the psyches of people of different racial groups. Not once before in my life had such an idea even crossed my mind. This idea was especially disconcerting to me because I am a poet and frequently use these words in this manner in my poems. How could people twist the simple use of imagery into racism? Whose mind could be so weak as to develop a complex over using colors in speech? It was a black day in the life of my intellectual development!

Prejudices have also changed their manifestation over the last several decades. We now see much more hatred directed by minorities, not only at whites, but at each other. No form of prejudice is good, but at least people of different groups are on an equal enough footing so we all experience it at times. Yet, I see a disturbing trend, what is called reverse racism. One of the more notable examples of this over the last several years has been the accusations in the Duke rape case. The press and racial activists jumped all over the boys the allegations were made against. They supposed that their privileged lifestyle as upper class whites had given them an air of invincibility. Yet, when the case was dropped how many apologies and recantations did we hear? How many of these accusers reexamined their prejudices that led them to convict these young men before their day in court? My bet is very few.

The double standard that applies in our society to what is acceptable for one group or another is disturbing. The use of the "N" word is just one example. As a teacher I have to deal with this on a near daily basis. I have to explain to all of my students that the word has no place in our vocabulary, no matter how it is used. I similarly despise the use of the "F" word directed at homosexual men. Its origin is derived from the burning of people alive. I don't care how one feels about any issue, but burning people alive is not a means of dealing with those with whom we disagree. I'd prefer a more civilized discussion or a debate.

We also see this double standard being used in more nefarious manners. The recent case of the "Jenna Six" is but one example. The nation was whipped up into a fury based on the manner in which these six young black men were supposedly treated. Many activists, of all colors, tried to make the case out to be one of the most grave injustices in human history. They alluded to lynchings and the likes of the Birmingham church bombing, yet when the facts of the case were investigated it was nothing of the sort. Yes, the young men in this case were overcharged, but to compare this to the true horrors of institutionalized racism is to dilute the struggle that blacks as a whole have faced in this country. Crying wolf on matters of race does nothing more than separate us even further as people. There is enough real racism and prejudice around to fight without manufacturing it.

One of the events I like to use to show the turning points of race relations in America is the first O.J. Simpson case. I don't care what one thinks of his guilt or innocence in the case; that is for God to judge. What I do care about is that it shows how far our country has come on these matters. How, you may be asking? The fact that O.J. was a rich black celebrity illustrates this point. When O.J. went to trial it became more important that he was a rich celebrity than that he was black. This is the first prominent case that showed how much more important it was that he was a rich celebrity. Ten years earlier and his blackness probably would have gotten him a conviction. Forty years ago he might not have even had a trial at all.

There is one issue that relates to race that causes extreme controversy; that issue is reparations. Usually this idea is applied to slavery in the United States. It also usually connotes reparations for blacks and blacks only. This completely ignores the fact that blacks were not the only group of people who were held as slaves in this country. It also ignores the fact that many groups faced oppression on a number of levels, and not all whites were beneficiaries of these horrible institutions. The concept that people of today can somehow correct the injustices of the past is essentially ridiculous. No measure we take in the present could remedy the pains endured years ago.

Too often this issue is put forth by liberals trying to curry political favor in our current time. Little thought is given to how gargantuan a task it would be to estimate what these reparations should be, who should get them, and who should pay for them. If blacks are entitled to reparations what does that mean for women, the Chinese, the Irish, Jews, Catholics, and a whole host of other groups? Where also is the consideration of the fact that those alive today are not the victims of slavery or these past prejudices? They may be indirectly affected, but who has not had some injustice perpetrated on someone at some point on their family tree? Reparations at this point will only hurt a new generation of innocent people and cause new tensions between people who exist today.

Not only is the idea of reparations bad in theory; it will be terrible in practice. Any attempt to designate certain groups to be punished for a crime that they did not commit is against the Fifth Amendment to the Constitution. How can I be made to pay for the offenses of another human being? Even if we try to relate the family benefits that one has gotten from historical injustices how would it be determined what penalty each person pays? My families were still back in Europe when this was going on. On top of that my family tree is quite diverse. Should the Irish and Catholic parts of me get reparations from the German/ Swiss Protestant part of me? Should the German part get reparations for the maltreatment received during the two world wars? And if I were somehow made to pay who should get that money? Will newly arrived Jamaican blacks get paid by U.S. reparations or should they be paid by their British beneficiaries? Should people of mixed race be forced to hand cash from their left to their right or the other way around? In fact, should lefties get some sort of compensation for their endurance of prejudice? And let's not forget the ambidextrous!

Hopefully that insane example is enough to get my point across. I have read editorials and books that suppose that all white people have benefited from the toils of slavery. This notion is not only offensive, but absurd. Yes, slavery aided in the economic development of this nation, but it is impossible to calculate its value. It is also impossible to calculate its cost. All of the racial tension, efforts to maintain the slave system, and cost to this nation in blood, can never be quantified in monetary terms. America has not had a perfect record when it comes to oppression. Save building a time machine there is little we can do in the present to alleviate the sufferings of the past.

The issue of so-called hate speech and hate crimes is also offensive to me. I mention it in my chapter on gay rights as well. We do not need hate speech and hate crime laws to protect our citizens. These offenses are already covered under verbal assault, intimidation, and other crimes. What I particularly don't like about these laws is their application. They are almost exclusively applied to whites. Yes, usually to whites that have acted like idiots, but people of other groups use hurtful words all the time. It is rare to see these laws applied when one is attacked due to the fact that they are white or a Christian. Hate laws are the exclusive product of the liberal mind, and they are usually only used when the target is in one of the groups that the left deems to have been oppressed. The liberals seem to only want to use these laws when it is the hated white man or Christian that has committed the offense. I don't want to see these laws applied at all. We need to use the statutes that cover these areas already. Punishing someone for what they think, no matter how ignorant, is not the American way.

One cannot forget the plight of the American Indian in the development of this country. I remember standing at a general store in South Dakota in 1991 just outside of Pine Ridge Indian Reservation. When I looked at the sign it had just been redone. The whole sign was repainted except the bottom. When I looked closer I could make out the words that had not been repainted. Those words said "No Indians." At the time I had never seen any people openly excluded from a store, no less with it painted on a sign. It was of little consolation to me that it wasn't repainted with the rest of the sign. The fact that it was there at all was what bothered me, but many Indian tribes have done well since then. They have turned their independent status into veritable gold mines with their establishment of casinos. Yet, these casinos may be what finally destroys their cultures in the end. I hope the wealth and prosperity these money-making machines bring won't cloud the sights of who they actually are.

This brings me to a more innocuous point: the renaming of sports teams from the high school to the professional level. Yes, I can see renaming a team if the name is totally offensive and has no redeeming quality, but some of the changes are so far out of line that it is ridiculous. Some team names that were actually meant to honor different groups have had moves made to change them. In my eyes there are much more salient points to attack in the battle on racism and prejudice. If you don't like the name then don't support the team. I, for one, happen to be a fan of Notre Dame. I also happen to be Irish. You don't see me whining and moaning that the team is called the Fighting Irish. Despite its duplicitous meaning I take pride in the Irish's fight and can chuckle at some of the more derogatory implications of the name. My character and worth are based on my own existence, not the name of a team.

Women in most of the cultures of the world have had a second class status throughout most of history. Our culture has had this problem as well. I feel it is a disservice to our society to take over half the populace and delegate them to an inferior position. Much has been done to remedy this unfortunate situation over the last hundred years. The difference between the oppression of women and other minorities is a bit different. Men and women are different, biologically and even to some degree in personality. We all know a man when we see one, we also know a woman when we see one. We have certain expectations of what they will be like, yet the problem comes when we actually try to define what those qualities are. Rather than do that I feel the best course is to allow our society to open up opportunities to both sexes and let the chips fall where they may.

I think that the liberals use race in ways in which they shouldn't. Even if they are attempting to lift up downtrodden groups their efforts have the opposite affect. Their constant use of race, gender, and ethnicity only serve to put light on the differences we have, rather than our similarities. There are many methods we can use that do not use quotas and special treatment to maintain diversity. The best means of doing this is establishing a meritocracy. If we would simply allow those that excel the most in any arena to ascend to their proper position the rest will take care of itself. Making special allowances for one group over another only causes the suspicion of their abilities. It is also contrarian to the purposes for which this nation was founded. A truly great America can only come from the unfettered exposition of the talents that God has given all of our citizens.

SMOKING, FATTY FOODS, AND LIBERAL FASCISTS

This is an issue that exposes the liberal mentality but also reveals that some conservatives deep down, when it comes to things that they don't like, are willing to dispense with freedom. Over the course of the last decade we have seen a sweeping change across the planet. Smoking is under attack and the self-righteous nanny state left has been leading the charge. As if that wasn't bad enough they have started to add fatty foods to their list of untouchable products. No thought is given to freedom or the right of self-determination, just the idea that it is somehow the government's right to control what people put into their bodies. Most of those who support these bans see themselves as some sort of health police. They believe that they are heroes saving ignorant folk from killing themselves. I have a few choice words for these self-proclaimed do gooders, but I'm trying to keep my book fit for young people. These know-it-alls better stop before it's something that they like to consume that is put into the taboo category.

Almost any product can be made to seem dangerous. Almost anything not consumed in moderation can lead to health problems. Even water can kill if it is drunk in significant enough quantities. The burden of proof needs to be placed on those who wish to remove the rights of citizens to make their own choices. Instead we see the proclamation that something is unhealthy and the fascists begin their campaign to eliminate whatever it is from the marketplace. Smoking was first on the chopping block due to the fact that it is unquestionably bad for our health, but now we see this idea being expanded to go after other products and ingredients. How long until this comes to the point where the government will monitor our individual diets and lifestyles? I'm not joking or exaggerating here: Once we allow for the government intrusion into any arena of our lives their power to interfere in our freedom to choose builds like a snowball rolling down a steep hill. The evidence for this concept can be seen when we look at the IRS, the public schools, the state motor vehicle agencies, and countless other cases where the government has been granted undue authority.

Let's first take a look at the anti-smoking fascists. They have waged a campaign to remove smoking from all public venues. They try to proclaim that they are waging this war on behalf of the non-smokers' subjection to second-hand smoke. Yet, the prohibitions that they have turned into laws often go far beyond this legitimate purpose. Their belief that smoking is an absolute evil has led them to far exceed the health of those who don't use tobacco. Those who support these laws feel that they are superior to those who smoke and therefore their work is righteous. They also fail to recognize how their sweeping ban on smoking is an infringement on the rights of smokers and the proprietors of privately owned businesses. Shouldn't the choice to have smoking in a private establishment be the right of the individual who owns it?

To show how these anti-smoking laws violate the rights of individuals all we have to do is give a few examples. In my home state of New Jersey, prior to our public smoking ban, we had only a handful of bars and restaurants that were a hundred percent smoke-free; virtually all the other establishments were mixed with smoking and non-smoking sections. If the real choice of the people was to have this all-encompassing ban would not most of the businesses been non-smoking? New York City was one of the first places in the country that caved into the anti-smoking fascists. In New York City the prohibition on smoking has taken on a truly totalitarian tone since the anti-smoking crusader

Mike Bloomberg became Mayor. There used to be a time when one could go to the outer parts of the open-air Yankee Stadium stairwells and have a cigarette. One might miss an important play in the game, but we had a place to light up that was away from others who did not want to be exposed to second-hand smoke. How was this hurting anyone but the smokers themselves?

Yet, the management of the team has made it that smoking anywhere in the stadium is cause for ejection. I now find myself hoping the game doesn't run too long or go into extra innings, but some other smokers have taken to getting a few drags when in the bathroom and now they are constantly filled with smoke. Due to this all the non-smokers are being subjected to second-hand smoke they weren't being exposed to prior to this draconian rule. Some localities across the nation have gone even a step further. They now want to ban smoking on the street or in apartment buildings and condo complexes. If the threshold for our effect on other people's health becomes this low there is no limit to what the government can ban or regulate or where they can do it. All of these examples point out that the basis for these anti-smoking regulations far exceeds the rights of non-smokers to remain free from breathing second-hand smoke. They also represent a dangerous extension of the power of the government.

It's also not enough for these crusaders to limit what we do indoors; they now want to extend the ban to the outdoors. In many communities there have been proposals to force smokers to light up a given distance from any establishment's entrance. In some cases the distances given effectively make a ban on smoking anywhere because the amount of space between storefronts is less than the stated amount of feet in the regulation. Nothing annoys me more when I'm out and some smug non-smoker gives me a dirty look because I'm standing outside having a cigarette. It's not enough that I've been kicked out into the street, but now they don't want me to smoke anywhere near a building. Again, if this is the ludicrous threshold that is being established in terms of how we affect others then there is nothing that the government won't have the power to control.

Now the absurdities of the health police are being carried even further. Again, the crusaders of New York City are leading the way. The omnipotent government of the city has now deemed trans-fats to be fit for prohibition. All eating establishments are not able to cook using oils that contain these compounds. The health of the citizens was put forward as the basis for this policy. Yet, I have never seen in the Constitution where it says that the government is supposed to manage the types of food I choose to eat. If someone wants French fries cooked in trans-fats then that is their right. To suggest anything else is to lift the state into a position of absolute power. Determining the menu and preparation of food is not the prerogative of the government, but of the proprietor of any given business.

One of the main reasons given by the health police is that those who are partaking of these unhealthy food and habits are a burden on the healthcare system. Using this logic we could ban or control just about any behavior or item. Wouldn't those without automobiles be able to ban the use of vehicles due to their exhaust? Wouldn't those without cell phones be able to demand that they be banned because of the dangerous light waves used to make their transmissions? Wouldn't the government have the power to monitor people's sex lives to ensure that they are not engaged in any activities that put them at risk of sexually transmitted diseases? The list could go on and on, but these examples prove the point. Once we open this Pandora's box the power of the government would be unbounded. They came after the smokers and I said nothing because I didn't smoke. They came after those who ate fatty foods and I said nothing because I ate a healthy diet. They went after those who didn't exercise and I said nothing because I led an active life. They came after those who ate red meat and I said nothing because I didn't like beef. And when they came after me there was no one left to speak up. Freedom usually slips away in increments, not in a single wave.

Ultimately this issue comes down to a matter of choice a matter of freedom. Business owners should be allowed to choose whether or not someone smokes in their establishment. Proprietors should be allowed to prepare their food in any manner they see fit, so long as it is sanitary. Stadiums should be able to provide isolated alcoves where smokers can have a cigarette without bothering other individuals. As it stands now all it does is push the diehard smokers into the bathroom for a puff and everybody who uses the facilities ends up breathing in smoke. Typical to the liberal their answer has been to ban, pass laws, and suppress the true freedom of citizens to make their own decisions about how they live their lives. Who, except for those morally opposed to smoking, wouldn't want to invest in an airline that allowed smoking on all its flights? We need to address these issues with common sense not absolutism.

The liberal fascists often point toward the individual rights of non-smokers. This is a fair point to make, but only when my choice is impeding on their rights. When means can be found that accommodate all of us then the law should permit it. We hear heart-wrenching tales about the poor waitress that has to breathe second-hand smoke. Emotional appeals to the plight of children getting obese because of McDonald's and soda. Yet, we hear little about the responsibility that adults are supposed to exercise in their personal lives. If the waitress doesn't want to breathe in second-hand smoke then she should find a job at a smoke-free restaurant. If little Tommy is getting fat then it is Mom, Dad, or the guardians' responsibility to do something about it. The government does not exist to be our omniscient parental surrogate. We are grown adults, and Americans; we have the right to make decisions for ourselves.

This liberal tyranny will have no end if it is not stopped now. The reasoning for these government impositions has no bounds. This line of logic can be used to justify any government intrusion into our personal lives. Smoking is one of the worst decisions that I have ever made. If I could go back in time and choose differently I would, but it is my right to do it so long as I don't impose it on others. Remember that the basis for these laws can be applied to anything; just because it is applied to something you may not like does not make it right. Furthermore, if the liberals were to ever succeed at establishing a national healthcare system they could use this idea to control every aspect of our daily lives. Imagine government-controlled diets, exercise regimens, and the monitoring of our minute-to-minute activities. When government takes power over anything it always looks to find ways to expand it. Today it's smoking; tomorrow it might be how much time you spend in the sun.

ILLEGAL IMMIGRATION

Illegal immigration has become a significant problem in the U.S. over the past few decades. This is largely due to the lax enforcement of the law. It is also due to the political opportunism of the two major parties. Support of industry and business to maintain an inexpensive pool of labor has lead Republicans, and some Democrats, to maintain the status quo. The hope of legalizing a large group of voters who are perceived to be in favor of the Democratic party has guided the left's positions on this issue. Added to these two political motivations is the reality that two decades of unfettered access to the U.S. has allowed at least twelve million people to work their way into the fabric of our society. It must be recognized that the policies and inaction of the past has created many messy social situations that will need to be addressed if we are to solve this problem, the most important of which is the manner in which we deal with families who are composed of illegal guardians and citizen minors. Many on the left try to make this issue about xenophobia and racism, particularly claiming it is aimed at Hispanics. This does not accurately portray the truths of this issue but more their prejudiced notion that the only aliens here illegally are Hispanic. The "undocumented" hail from six continents and possibly seven if one includes penguins from Antarctica.

Many believe that an amnesty for those who have already been here is a fair idea. As nice as that may sound, that is as impractical as the physical deportation of the multitudes already here illegally. Even if the lowest estimate of twelve million is used we have to consider the ripple effect that this will have. With legalization comes the privilege of bringing family members to the United States. This will swell the number of those gaining legal residence, using the extremely conservative number of fifteen million; that is a 5% jump in our total population in one shot. Not to mention the probability that this will increase the perception that if one comes here illegally just wait twenty years or so and an amnesty will be declared.

The overall solution to this problem is simple. The best way to deal with the problem is to take away the incentive that draws people to our country, even at the cost of breaking the law. That incentive is obvious: money. It is impractical, and unnecessary, to go after the illegal immigrants. The best way to remove this incentive is to go after employers who knowingly hire people without the legal status to be here. Take away the ability to work and all future illegal immigration would be virtually nullified. The best way to accomplish this would be to have a tiered system of punishment for employers. First offenses can be met with a general fine, second offenses with a fine for each illegal alien employed, and finally third offenses could include jail time. Illegal immigrants can't live here without a job.

Those who have no social ties to the United States would find their way home. For those who could not afford to return to their country of origin I would even suggest that the government pay for or provide the means for them to do so. This might include the consideration of using military air and sea transport at no cost to those being repatriated. The logistics of such a program could be worked out on a country by country basis. Countries that refuse to cooperate could be held accountable with some form of sanction; those that agree to work with us could be given priority to their citizens in any guest worker programs we have or that will be created.

I understand the harshness of the poverty that drives people to come to America. I can even grasp how this supersedes the willingness to abide by the law. Yet, our country cannot take on the burden of the entire world's poor by allowing them all to come here; to do so would be suicide. Our economy is the largest in the world. We do have a need to have some sort of legal programs that admit migrant and temporary workers. In many cases these programs already exist and they can be expanded and improved as needed.

Now the really difficult social aspects of any methods we implement to deal with this problem need to be discussed. I have already mentioned the problem of dealing with families that are part legal, illegal, and in many cases part citizen. What I have not mentioned is the severe problems of gangs, crime, and the cross-border drug trade. All of these issues need to be looked at individually. Lastly there is the need to determine how the security of our borders and points of entry can be exploited by our enemies. Namely, Al Qaeda, and the specter of terrorism as a whole.

Again, I will deal with the easiest of the problems that lay before us. Our criminal justice system is broken when we see how it operates with our own citizens. It becomes even more dysfunctional when we consider how we deal with illegal aliens. Sanctuary cities and perverse restrictions on how illegals are to be identified, processed, and adjudicated, exacerbate the ability of our legal system to handle the myriad cases that come before it. First and foremost it is time that we recognize that the mere presence of someone in the United States does not convey upon that individual the full rights of an American citizen. I know this may be difficult for the likes of the ACLU and the radical left to comprehend, but it is the truth.

How many crimes have been committed by people here illegally who have already had serious encounters with the law and yet remain free to roam our streets? How many illegals serve time and then are returned to our communities rather than to their homeland? How many illegal aliens with known gang and criminal affiliations are allowed to remain in our country? The duty of this government is to protect the lives, liberty, and property of American citizens first. To suggest that our Constitution and its framers had any other consideration is ludicrous.

Clearly, the borders and entry points into the U.S. are a security nightmare. From unchecked cargo ships to long stretches of unguarded frontier on both the Canadian and Mexican border to inadequately monitored airports our nation is not that difficult to enter. Technology can greatly reduce our vulnerability in all of these areas. Yet, some more concrete measures also need to be considered. Personally I have a great distaste for walls and fences due to their cost, symbolism, and environmental impacts, but in some more heavily trafficked areas these may need to be utilized. We can't forget how easy it is to cross some areas of the Great Lakes and St. Lawrence River by boat. The truly determined can always find some way across the vast expanses of water and land that outline this beautiful country. We must be able to marshal the resources we have at hand and integrate federal and state agencies. We also have to strengthen our law enforcement capabilities so that those who do enter illegally can not operate as easily as they have been able to in the past.

This leads to the next logical step in any plan to address security, documentation and use of public services. Closing these loopholes in our system addresses both those illegally here for jobs and those here to do us harm. Licenses and permits for driving must be only for those who can prove they are here legally. Many of the hijackers who committed the attacks on 9/11 had multiple legal forms of U.S. identification. How can law enforcement agents adequately perform their duty when faced with such obstacles to recognizing with whom they are dealing? Furthermore it is necessary to insist that those who are attempting to use our public schools and government agencies show their legal residence in order to gain access to such institutions and programs. For the sake of humanity I do believe it is best to forgo the same requirements in our emergency rooms and healthcare facilities.

Now the hardest of the problems that we face when addressing the presence of millions of illegal aliens in this country is the intertwined relationships they have with many who are legal. This is particularly a constitutional problem when someone here illegally is the guardian of someone who is a citizen. Believe it or not, there are also many adult immigrants who are here because their parents took them into this country illegally many years ago. Even though this percentage of people is not great their numbers are significant. Rather than try to assess how large a group this is I feel it is constitutionally required and morally necessary to try to find some way to justly accommodate these people who did not put themselves in to this position by their own design. I say that this is the hardest part of this problem to solve because it has the most potential to be abused, not only by those illegally here trying to manipulate the system, but by politicians trying to do the same as well.

Lastly I feel insulted when hundreds of thousands, maybe millions, of people march on our streets demanding rights, this, despite the fact that they are not here legally. These rallies only prove the ineptness of our legal system and the irony that those who have broken our laws can demand rights under our legal system. What sovereign nation can exist under such hypocrisy?

LIBERALS HAVE IRAQNIPHOBIA

This chapter is one of the most important in this book. It may also be the most difficult to adequately address. The vast array of countries and players in the War on Terror complicates the ability to look at all of the issues involved in a direct manner. Each theatre of the war has its connection to all of the others. When addressing Iraq one cannot forget about Iran. When addressing Iran one cannot forget about the role of Russia, and so on and so forth. This makes any discussion on how to enact U.S. foreign policy a nightmare. Unlike the way I treated the environment, I feel it is best in this situation to deal with most of these issues in a single chapter. Since September 11th almost all foreign policy is inextricably intertwined.

I feel the easiest place to begin on the War on Terror is where the most agreement can be found, Afghanistan. 9/11 brought the reality of terror to our shores. It also magnified the failings of our foreign policy in the decades leading to the attacks, and our inability to grasp who and what our enemies are. I am as guilty of this short-sightedness as anyone else. I remember laughing at Osama Bin Laden when he read his fatwa of war against the "Great Satan," the United States, in the late 1990s. I also remember asking rhetorically, "What's some guy in a cave in Afghanistan going to do to America?"

Several years later I found out. In the intervening years I had learned enough about Al Qaeda and world events to know that the acts of 9/11 were the works of these terrorists if it wasn't done by some domestic group, yet I was still totally surprised by the scale of destruction we endured on that day. Living in the New York City area only amplified my connection to this historic event. Wondering about the safety of loved ones and watching the city burn with my own eyes had a profound affect on me. I feel it is safe to say my outlook on the world was forever changed. If you had asked me on September 10th, 2001 if I thought we should invade Afghanistan I would have said, "No!" On September 11th my answer to that question became, "Yes!"

The events of that day resonate frequently for me. Every time I approach New York City I notice the gaping hole where those towers used to stand. I remember the plume of smoke that was visible for nearly two months rising up from Ground Zero. I remember standing in Montclair, N.J., overlooking the city that afternoon listening to the sound of sirens in the distance heading toward the war zone those bastards made of lower Manhattan. I remember wondering how some of my friends and loved ones who were in the city were faring. I was lucky none of them were close enough to the World Trade Center to have been injured, but many others did not have the same luck as me that day. Even as I write this, more than six years later, my eyes well up with tears and I get angry!

Now, back to the thought of a place where most of us can find agreement, Afghanistan. I remember when the Taliban blew up some giant statues of Buddha shortly before we were attacked by Al Qaeda. As a historian I thought that this was the epitome of idiocy. I also felt what a great shame it was to have lost such grand cultural icons to posterity, but it wasn't enough in my mind to justify war. Yet, America and the rest of the world turned its back on the horrific theocracy of the Taliban. We failed to understand the significance of allowing ideological enemies to find safe harbor in another nation. We failed to recognize that people who espouse the destruction of another actually mean it. We did not see that the Islamo-Fascists were at war with us, but we weren't at war with them. We treated terror as a policing operation, not a war. Don't get me wrong: At the time I had a similar outlook on the matter. To this day I will still defend much of Bill Clinton's actions on terror by simply reminding people of the mindset the world had before September 11th.

Those excuses no longer hold water in the post-9/11 world. Appeasement or weakness now can only mean certain death.

Few people objected to the invasion of Afghanistan. Even most of the left felt this to be necessary. We understood the errors of our ways and recognized that we had no choice but to oust the Taliban and go after Al Qaeda. By and large, the world community supported these operations and they still mostly do today. We also can see the same support given by foreign governments and intelligence agencies today when it comes to hunting down individual terrorists, but somehow this assistance fades into opposition when we pose this fight as a general ideological conflict. Whenever the U.S. and our few true allies act on this idea as policy the world's backing of us disappears. I feel that this occurs largely due to the way in which liberals view the world. They compartmentalize evil and fail to realize the truth of the adage that the enemy of my enemy can be my friend. This is how they can believe that the secular nature of Saddam Hussein would be enough to prevent him from working with terror groups. This is where the divide on how to conduct the war on terror truly becomes evident.

Islamo-fascism is an ideology. It has roots in almost every country in the world. Though it is not the belief system of all Muslims it is based on a warped interpretation of the Q'ran. It is also able to find commonality with others who view the West as a threat. This not only applies to leaders like Saddam Hussein, but to fringe elements of the left within our own society that view capitalism with disdain and the Western world as historically evil. Terrorists will ignore their beliefs if it means they can kill us. Remember, their goal is to make us Muslims in exactly the way they see fit or make us dead. That is it: When we are dealing with these religious fascists we must never forget that there are only two options. They will settle for nothing less. Liberals seem to think there is some room for compromise, that there is something short of war that will assuage these fanatics.

Others held these views in the leadup to WWII. The infamous Neville Chamberlain, Prime Minister of Great Britain, thought he could negotiate peace with Hitler. Many Americans thought we could sit safely apart from the likes of Imperial Japan and Nazi Germany protected by two oceans. The world today is even smaller, and if it wasn't true then it certainly isn't true today. Had the world listened to Winston Churchill and stopped Germany in the mid-1930s maybe several thousand might have died instead of the tens of millions that died in WWII. I liken the method that we are currently fighting the War on Terror to what could have been done back then. Although we have made mistakes in the present conflict, I believe our actions are preventing our enemies from getting greater strength and are actually limiting casualties instead of increasing them. War is always terrible, but what would we be facing had we not stopped Saddam Hussein? Liberals seem to only focus on what could have been done better, or different, not on what we need to do today and even tomorrow.

I understand that Saddam Hussein had little, or nothing, to do with 9/11. Yet, I do believe he was doing everything in his power to get his hands on weapons of mass destruction. I also believe it is quite probable that he did have them. Even if he didn't, why did he refuse to comply with the weapons inspections? Why did most of the intelligence agencies of the world believe he had them? Did we not give him months to dispose, hide, or move the weapons before we invaded? I don't want to rehash the entire Iraq conflict for the forty-billionth time, but similarly to the leeway I give Bill Clinton for his inaction in the 1990s I point to the mindset of the world in 2002 and 2003. I will go even further: Knowing what I know now, despite our myriad mistakes, if I could go back in time I would still invade Iraq. The world is infinitely better off today because of it. Only history can prove me right. We can't take chances with maniacal dictators and WMDs!

The current Iraq war has many lessons. One is, with the exception of the first Persian Gulf War, the U.S. and our Western allies have not fought a war the right way since WWII. Exit strategies and absurdly restrictive rules of engagement only serve to allow our enemy to have greater strength than they actually possess. Limiting conflicts within a particular nation's borders is also an idiotic way of waging war. Today Iran and Syria are the Laos and Cambodia of Iraq. How can we fight effectively when nearby countries are used as staging grounds to attack our forces in Iraq? No less, with the permission and encouragement of those countries' respective regimes. And then there is the press, the media. I have no problems with the idea of reporting on a war, but if we had such representations of conflict as we do now during WWII we would have lost or withdrawn from the war. We can't maintain public support if every mistake we make is amplified and every kitten killed in an air raid is broadcast across the world the next morning with some teary-eyed journalist standing over its body. War is terrible! It can't be fought completely cleanly or with perfect precision. Innocents get killed and that is just a matter of fact. Of course, we have to do the utmost to prevent this, but we should not fight a war with both our hands tied behind our back.

This insane hope of fighting wars in this unnecessarily restrictive manner is a product of the left. We first see its shadow in the likes of Woodrow Wilson during and after WWI. We see it also in the Geneva Conventions and the Kellogg-Briand Pact. Its ultimate futility is embodied in the international organizations the League of Nations and the U.N. Neither ever accomplished their goals and both have only proven how ineffective world bodies can be when they allow despots and tyrants to sit as equals at the negotiating table. The problem with these notions is that the liberals presuppose their values onto all other people. Their ultimate failure is the inability to see that freedom and the rights of man will never be recognized by zealots who believe that their way of life should be the only one.

The current Iraq conflict also allows us to see just how far the left will go in order to oppose the war. It is one thing to have opposition, it is quite another to undermine our war effort as it is being fought. Liberals seem more interested in proving the Bush administration's incompetence than in making Iraq a stable country we can return to the Iraqis. Every single mistake is trumpeted and excoriated by the liberal media and the Democrats in Congress. Harry Reid said publicly that the war was lost while our troops were still fighting on the battlefield. Many Democrat senators moaned for years how Bush had sent in too few troops to do the job, and when he initiated the surge they turned around and opposed that. We didn't talk about troop reductions in WWII until Berlin and Tokyo capitulated. We can't win a war when we keep telling the enemy that we're just about ready to turn around and go home, especially a war with fanatic religious fascists. The left's opposition to the war seems more like a mental illness against Bush and his administration rather than a genuine response to what has occurred in Iraq. Their flailing and contorted positions only serve to reinforce this concept.

Liberals have also done their best to impede our efforts to fight the War on Terror in every way possible. The ACLU repeatedly attacks any effort to improve our surveillance of those that may want to do harm to us in our country. Under the guise of civil rights and privacy they try to restrict the efforts of authorities to get information on terrorists. Yes, I feel some of the moves by the Bush Administration may have gone a little over the line, but if we were to listen the left we would think that we have had millions of citizens rounded up and thrown into gulags. Yet, Code Pink and Cindy Sheehan are still free to roam the streets protesting our government's actions. ACLU lawyers have access to the courts and, if my memory serves me correctly, hundreds of thousands of people marched down the streets of New York City to demonstrate their opposition to the war. We are fighting a group of people who use societal stealth, our own laws, and asymmetrical warfare to attack us. The government has to have some leverage in order to pursue these enemies. When our laws are improperly used by our authorities, recourse in the courts is still an effective means to right injustice.

This same mindset is exemplified in the attempts by the left to apply the rights of the Geneva Conventions to non-uniformed terrorists caught on the battlefields of Iraq and Afghanistan, and others captured in the War on Terror. These terrorists do not meet any of the standards that establish one as a legal combatant. Yet, the liberals want to give these people public trials in the U.S. under our Constitution. Rights of American citizens have never been applied to legal combatants, no less to those who are fighting a covert war against us. One example proves this to be true. Major John Andre of the British Army during our Revolution was caught without a uniform with the plans that Benedict Arnold had given him. Did Washington order a trial, did he hold him prisoner? No, he was hanged on the spot as a spy. The scum we are fighting now certainly deserve no better treatment. This is especially true when so many that we have released from places like Guantanamo Bay have been recaptured on the battlefield again. The jihadists aren't going to have an epiphany and go home and be nice. If they are willing to sacrifice their own women and children in the course of their attacks I doubt many of them are going to cease until they meet their goal of seeing Allah, and we should do everything in our power to assist them in attaining this goal.

So often I hear liberals use the argument that fighting terror only creates more terrorists. I hear them say that it's our actions on the world stage that cause these people to fight us. Yet, when they are pressed to come up with an alternative it is either silence or we hear ideas like diplomacy and sitting down to talk with our enemies. Truly I wish these ideas were practical, but they are not. We were attacked before we invaded Iraq. Their children have been inculcated with a hatred of the West for at least the last several decades. We have made many of these countries rich by buying their oil, yet somehow, no matter what, we are still the enemy.

Let's be clear: I am speaking of the radicals in the Islamic world who preach hate. It is these religious fascists who will always hate us. They hate our freedom, our democracy, our openness, and the rights of our women. They dream of a seventh-century world and we do not fit into that paradigm. We are the Great Satan and Israel is the Little Satan. They need a convenient scapegoat for their followers to hate. Their hatred of us is the base of their power. We are the source of all their misery and every problem in their midst; if we were only gone all would be right with the world, according to them. If you can find a way to negotiate with that, I'd be happy to listen.

Very often arguments are made that we would be better off spending the money from the Iraq war on terrorism prevention methods here at home. I don't think that these two ideas need to be mutually exclusive. Obviously the question of cost does make it difficult to do both to the extent we would need.

Personally I think this is one of the better ideas posited by those who are against the war. Yet, I feel the extreme limitations that our extensive borders and infrastructure place on the ability of technology and manpower to adequately defend us makes the War on Terror necessary. It would be ideal to invest in better security at our ports of entry and our borders. We have already witnessed the dramatic increase of security at our airports and similar efforts need to be taken elsewhere. Rather than discuss specifics here, I believe studying the tools to do this should be done by those who operate these facilities and borders. Cost-effectiveness and reliability should be given the highest priority in determining what we use to enhance our security.

We must not only fight those who want to kill us, but those who seek to educate another generation in this ideology. To do this we will need more than bombs and guns. I believe that some of the liberals may be pointing to this idea when they speak of talking or diplomacy, but it is a lot easier said than done. On top of this we need to have a recognition of how the cultures that produce our enemies think. If we retreat and allow ourselves to be attacked without response they will perceive this as weakness. This will only further serve to stiffen their perception of us as a bankrupt people. Yet, I still do hold out the hope that education and cultural interchange programs can aid in showing these potential enemies that they have nothing to fear from us. Soccer games and sharing a falafel can go a long way. Look what chocolate, cigarettes, and baseball did for our enemies after WWII.

I hate war, but sometimes we must fight. It is hard to tell just what percentage of liberals happens to believe this. From the way the left has acted in this war I'd have to say that the number must be fairly low. Whether by intention or incident the left has done almost everything it can to impede our effort to fight and increase our enemies' ability to attack us. I have seen history twisted, positions changed for political expedience, legal attempts to inhibit our war effort, and out-and-out lies. Never in American history has such an effort been made with such cynical purposes behind them. Vietnam was close, but I think the war in Iraq takes the top position.

THE ENVIRONMENT

This issue carries so many different facets to it I am going to separate some of the larger issues into chapters of their own. In the case of the environment as a whole some may be surprised by the manner in which I believe true conservatives should take the issue. I'll start out by pointing out that the root word of conservative is conserve. I'd also like to point out that the word in the Bible often translated as dominion, from God gave us "dominion" over the land, would better be translated as stewardship. I feel there is great importance in these two words. They lead to the understanding that God gave us this Earth to watch over, to conserve. Dominion is derived from the Latin *dominus*, meaning lord. Its connotation in English is absolute power or control. Stewardship has the connotation that we shall only watch over the Earth for a time and that we'd better return it to our Lord in a state that he would be pleased with. Being that God said he notices when the least sparrow falls, I feel that we best maintain our Earth in a way that preserves what God has created.

In addition to the first point I made I would like to add my own unique perspective when it comes to viewing issues that concern the environment. Amongst the many passions in life that I have it seems I have been given a genetic disposition towards the love of plants and trees. At the risk of sounding conceited I must say that I have been blessed with quite a green thumb. Not only is this personal, but it seems to run on one side of my family. Farming, working with trees and plants, and gardening seem to be quite a passion with my mother, grandfather, and great grandfather, all of whom I have been close with during my life. Their interactions with me have given me a strong feeling for the natural world and greenery in particular.

Another of my great passions has also been meteorology. I have always enjoyed weather, specifically, severe weather. Lightning, snow, wind, rain, fog, thunder—in short, any weather that exudes the power and imposition of nature. I have chased hurricanes, tornadoes, and have savored every storm or bit of inclement weather that has passed me by throughout my life. Moreover, I have studied and recorded the weather and climate since I was about eleven years old. This has not been limited to my own environment or time, but to the world and its past as a whole.

Finally, I would like to point out that science has been an interest and part of my profession. I am a high school teacher. Among the subjects that I teach is environmental science. Clearly this does not bestow upon me the title of expert, but it certainly does permit me the right to claim a familiarity with the issues that concern the environment. Essentially, environmental science is the study of mankind and our interaction with the eco-systems of the world. Ultimately, this is the science that tries to find the ways that society can coexist with the natural world, the science that strikes the balance between what we do to the environment and how we get what we need to survive.

What I have seen and studied leads me to believe that we do have a serious crisis in the natural world. And anyone with common sense knows that we cannot live without a stable environment. Yet, I shudder at the extremism of the radical environmentalists and the likes of Al Gore. I detest the notions of those who compare the worth of animals and plants with the souls of human beings. I despise the idea that somehow the West should be punished for its past use of fossil fuels and that the developing nations can pollute all they want. The Kyoto treaty so trumpeted by the so-called environmentalists was nothing more than a ploy to eviscerate the developed world and destroy the capitalist economies as a whole. Carbon credits, globalism, and the United Nations' pronouncements on global warming are all just means to an end, an end that I am hard-pressed to explain without believing that the ultimate goal of the proponents of such ideas is the destruction of the very civilization in which we live.

All politics aside, there are a myriad of problems facing the environment. The real question is how we prioritize the solutions. Which issues are the most pressing and which solutions are most practical? Many environmental problems can be addressed by not doing particular activities and others can be eliminated by changing behaviors. Obviously, laws and regulations have to play a role, but we must beware that we do not destroy national sovereignty and the rights of individuals as a whole. The danger in using the government, both national and international, to legislate the solution to all environmental issues is the creation of a tyranny, a tyranny that will have the laws built on the interests of those who write them. This is already evidenced in the U.N.'s attempts to deal with these issues.

Climate change is probably the most significant environmental problem. The underlying human contribution to this problem is our means of energy production and deforestation. Even if natural forces are the main cause of climate change it would be helpful for us to modify the impact we have on the environment. I will examine global climate change and energy usage in their own chapters. Yet, I will have to touch upon them here as well.

Every problem with the environment has social, political, moral, and economic components that need to be addressed in order to find a solution. It is easy to say stop deforestation, but quite another to tell poor people in the Amazon to starve rather than use slash and burn techniques to feed themselves with subsistence farming. We can dream of an economy based on renewable energy, but how do we make the transition from fossil fuels? What do we do when our new technologies have unintended environmental affects? I can already foresee major problems that we will face in the disposal of spent solar panels with their high levels of silicon and other substances. Brazil moved to an economy mostly based on bio-fuels and now they face nitric acid in the atmosphere from these alternative fuels. I am not saying that these challenges mean we should do nothing, just that we need to anticipate the environmental effects from any change that we make on a large scale. Nature is very well balanced and any alteration will tip that balance in new directions.

I have no problem with the idea that we are all responsible as individuals. I have planted dozens of trees that have survived, but I must admit I did it more because I like trees and simply think they should cover every inch we can possibly give them. Mind you that I live in New Jersey and that this area should be forested while other natural areas should be maintained with their indigenous vegetation. What is often not recognized is that people are part of our eco-systems. So long as we exist we will be trying to strike a balance between our use of the environment and our impact on it.

New Jersey is the most densely populated state in the union. Yet, our population of deer and bears are extremely dense as well. Deer are particularly destructive to the forest when they exist in large numbers. Their voracious appetite essentially cleans out all of the underbrush and young trees, diminishing the woodlands' ability to replace itself in the future. The problem is that the deer have few natural predators. I do not foresee the introduction of wolves and coyotes in numbers significant enough to manage the overpopulation of deer. Yet, every attempt to hunt deer is met with extreme opposition from animal rights advocates. They portray hunters as vicious, bloodthirsty murderers lying in wait to blow Bambi's brains out and claim all hunting is done as a sick form of fun. I don't hunt, but every hunter I have ever known has been a strong supporter of maintaining our natural environment. They have also used every part of the carcass they possibly could.

The problem of bears in New Jersey can also serve as an example of environmental extremism. Estimates of the number of bears in the state vary greatly, usually between 1,500 and 3,000. Despite the fact that I support efforts to live with the bears in and of themselves they do not seem to be totally solving the problem. I have been chased by a bear while hiking. Numerous attacks have been reported in much of the state. Yet, any attempt to allow a limited hunt is met with extreme protest, usually coming from people who live in urban areas unaffected by the bears. These people do not have to worry every time they let their pets or children set foot outdoors.

If we face this many difficulties in dealing with local issues, how much more difficult will it be to cope with national and international problems? Many of the problems in the third world are caused by the manner in which the poor live off of the land. Any attempt to maintain forests and natural eco-systems has to allow for the adjustments that these people will have to make in the way they live their everyday lives. Yet, these obstacles pale in comparison to how the industries that support the lifestyles of the developed world affect the environment. We consume by far the most energy and natural resources per capita. This is especially true of the United States. We are about 5% of the world's population, yet, we consume nearly 25% of the energy used on planet Earth. No solution is possible without a significant change in our consumption. Personally, I believe this can be achieved primarily through voluntary and gradual change, but some form of collective action will have to be taken.

My problem with the left is in how they approach the dialogue about environmental issues. They seem to take an adversarial position and place all of the blame on big, bad, evil corporations. The course of action they take is to attack, attack, and attack. Yes, there are some sinister individuals who are willing to sacrifice human lives and the environment to profit, but they are in an extreme minority. In fact, it is the profit motive that can best engineer the necessary changes individuals and industry need to make in order to preserve the natural world and an inhabitable planet. Much of the waste in the industrialized world, and the U.S. in particular, comes from practices that we can alter or eliminate altogether. Rather than attack industry we need to work together to modify how our way of life disrupts the environment.

I also have a problem with limousine and private jet liberals. I find it ironic that the so-called "green" Oscars and U.N. meetings on global climate change are attended by people who primarily arrive on private jets and stretch limousines. They maintain their extravagant lifestyles and then tell everyone else how to live. I also detest the hypocrisy of carbon credits and offsets. If you want to reduce your "carbon footprint," plant your own damn trees. When was the last time one of these hypocrites got a callous in the garden turning over the soil or planting some flowers? I don't need carbon offsets. I do my own work.

I have heard some justify the alarmism about the environment and global climate change by saying it is necessary in order to get the public's attention on these issues. I find this to be a very dangerous position to take. If people have their attention drawn to the issue by exaggerated claims, what will happen to their perspective when they discover they have essentially been fooled or lied to? When we publicize the need to attack a problem one should use the least controversial figures to do so. This ensures that emotion does not govern science and policy. Furthermore, when exaggerations are exposed they will tend to discredit those who posited these notions in the first place.

We need to practically examine and investigate how society is impacting the environment. We need to find realistic and obtainable methods for reducing the negative effects that we have on the eco-systems in which we live. Americans have some specific problems that cause us to use more energy and pollute more than cultures similar to our own. Two such issues are our lack of reliable public transportation, excess packaging and unnecessary waste. Western Europe and Japan far exceed our utilization of mass transportation and they certainly do not have the same amount of waste from everyday living that we do. I hate to see the tremendous amount of garbage generated at barbeques, public functions, and businesses, specifically the use of disposable utensils, plates, and cups and the enormous amounts of biodegradable materials thrown into the trash. Plastics are made with oil. I find this to be a poor choice of how to manage a finite resource. Using plastic is fine, but using it one time and sending it to a landfill is just plain stupid.

Another area in which we should look to change our behaviors is in landscaping. Removing fallen leaves and vegetation from property will eventually deplete the soil. Those materials should be composted and returned to the same Earth from which they came whenever possible. Use of herbicides and pesticides also needs to be reduced. Do we really need to use Roundup on a single weed in a sidewalk crack? Fertilizers cause an abundance of plant growth in waterways, which cause them to be choked out. Lawnmowers, blowers, and other yard tools waste an enormous amount of fuel energy. Not to mention the incessant amount of noise they produce. I'm not saying these chemicals and tools have no place, but they certainly do not need to be used as much as they are. All of these issues also need to be addressed when we consider farming as well.

Deforestation is also a major problem. Selective cutting in natural areas is a very important method we should increasingly use to replace clear-cutting techniques. Tree farming and sustainable forest management have also got to be utilized to preserve our woodlands. Paper is one of the most significant uses we have for timber. Alternatives to wood pulp paper, such as hemp, have the potential to reduce our use of trees a great deal. Clearing forests for farming and ranching is no longer a viable option when we consider sensible uses of the land, except in a few extreme cases. Overall, we just simply need to use sustainable methods when harvesting wood.

This problem becomes more complex when looking at the third world. Slash and burn farming techniques, especially used in tropical areas, are a mainstay of many people already living at the margins of starvation. Use of wood for heating and cooking is also an inexpensive fuel for those who have little money. Aid to poor countries is a nice gesture, but they need to have self-sustaining industries that allow them to produce what they need for themselves. Micro-loans have had a significant impact on changing the lives of many in the poorest parts of the world. These are loans that are made directly to individuals rather than to national governments, which have had a tendency to waste this money on failed projects and lose much of the remaining capital to corruption and graft. Large projects do have a role in raising the living standard of those in developing nations—look at what the Aswan high dam has done for Egypt—but individuals best understand their local environment and economy, and their personal participation in deciding how they will find new ways to sustain themselves should be an integral part of any plan to reduce man's impact on the environment. Give a man a fish and you feed him for a day; teach him how to fish and he will be fed for a lifetime.

Recycling materials is also an effective use of our resources. This not only reduces our need to produce new materials, but eliminates a large portion of the waste we send to landfills. Unfortunately the use of recycling is not as prevalent as it should be. Local governments need to reinvigorate the programs that they have. In many places recycling programs have declined in their effectiveness. New Jersey in 2007 had a lower percentage of recyclable materials being recycled than it did ten years earlier. Such steps backward are unacceptable if we are to seriously hope that we can manage our impact on the environment.

Pollution control is also a very important issue. This ranges from factory and auto emissions to sewerage treatment and water contamination. I believe that a great deal has already been accomplished on these problems in the industrialized world, but much more needs to be done in the developing world. China is quickly encroaching on the U.S. when it comes to who produces the most emissions into the atmosphere.

Any attempt to address this problem needs to heavily concentrate on how to reduce the pollution of the developing world. This is why I feel that the Kyoto treaty was such a failure. It all but exempted half the world's population from taking any action on what they pump into the skies. Yes, the developing nations need special consideration, but they cannot have a free pass when it comes to pollution.

Preservation of species and eco-systems is a paramount concern when we look at the environment. Species may hold the keys to the development of medicines and other manmade materials. The totality of any eco-system also depends on the maintenance of the species that exist within it. Sometimes the loss of one species can produce a chain reaction that devastates an entire area. Every environment is a delicately balanced machine that works as a sum of its parts. The removal of any one part can have an impact on the system as a whole. This is not always catastrophic, but it has been at times in the past. One of the biggest threats along these lines is the potential loss of plankton in the oceans, due to increased ultra-violet light resulting from the loss of the ozone layer. It is also a moral issue when human activity contributes to the loss of a species. This is particularly evident when we look at the threats faced by so many of the large-sized animals across the planet. Virtually every big cat and great ape species is threatened or endangered. We need to do more to preserve them and the habitats in which they exist.

The world as we know it is in danger of disappearing. True wilderness is almost gone. Human society is affected by its own waste and practice. I believe we need to alter the ways in which we use the land, air, water, and natural resources necessary for our existence. Yet, I also know that we cannot simply overturn overnight the way the world operates without catastrophic results. This needs to be examined alongside the need to change. With sober observation and sound science we should be able to move our global community toward a balance between human needs and the preservation of the environment that will ensure a sustainable world.

GLOBALISM

Globalism goes by more than one name. One-worlders and internationalists are just two of the more common pseudonyms. I feel that the left has a large contingency that overtly and covertly supports this idea. Yet, it needs to be recognized that some on the right also support this concept. Globalism is one of the more esoteric dangers to the United States and the world. Our national sovereignty is threatened by this idea. It entices the sensibilities by its call to the oneness of our humanity. It hides behind the façade of international cooperation and equality, but its threat lies in the accumulation of power that comes with the organizations that will gain control if the globalists succeed. The main instrument that will be used to effect this concept will be the U.N. They will also be the main benefactor if internationalism comes to fruition.

Why am I so concerned about the institution of one-world government? Some of my concerns are political and cultural; these I will discuss here. Others, as a Christian, concern me in a religious manner. They will have to wait for another forum. When we look at this idea we need to look at what has happened in the last century and to the rise of the European Union. The establishment of the League of Nations, and later the U.N., are based on this concept as well. I know that many people do not see the same sinister specter in these organizations as I do, but that is mostly due to ignorance of their operations. The U.S. should never sign any agreement, or join any international body, that has jurisdiction above our laws. Even if we did it is unconstitutional and therefore illegal!

I have no problem with international organizations in and of themselves, but the inevitable abuse of such power is all too apparent. I also have great suspicion as to the motives of many of the proponents of these ideas. The contingent of the left that views the West as evil does not have our interest at heart. Some of them also seem to want to punish the West for its colonial past and our economic success. Not everyone that supports these ideas is necessarily conscious of what lay behind the efforts of globalists. Yet, many in these movements actively seek the destruction of the West as a whole, and particularly the United States. Ultimately they envision a world without borders with an enlightened bureaucratic body of elites determining what is best for people over the entire Earth.

Let's take a look at the case of the Kyoto treaty. Many across the globe cite the fact that the U.S. refused to sign this document as a failure of our country. I see it as a blessing that we did not endorse this agreement. It is based on a flawed concept. That concept is the idea that all nations should be held accountable for their CO_2 emissions past and present. It also exempts most of the developing world from reducing their future output of carbon dioxide. This may seem innocuous until one considers its implications. If we were to agree to this concept it would have tremendous impact on our economy. It also fails to consider the use of CO_2 in the past, and the fact that no serious consideration of this pollutant was raised until around 1970. Why should the U.S. put regulations on our economic life that other nations do not have to meet? I understand that a more gradual approach to reducing emissions needs to take place in the third world, but a total exemption? Any treaty on this issue must address the participating nations with as much equality as possible.

We in the U.S. are already experiencing difficulty maintaining manufacturing jobs within our borders. What would happen to our economy if we were to add restrictions on our industry that nearly half the world wouldn't have? This debacle has been repeated in the U.N.'s intergovernmental panel on climate change. The IPCC is a bureaucratic group that has based many of its' remedies to climate change on suspect science. They have also continued in the tradition of Kyoto. Consistently international bodies put the brunt of cost and sacrifice at the door of the West, especially America. I am tired of working with international bodies that do not have our interest, and often hold deep antipathy for my country in their hearts.

If you look at the inner workings of the U.N. it seems they spend most of their time debating and the rest of the time hating. The world body's hatred of the U.S. and Israel is particularly notorious. Israel is berated time and time again, but hardly a whisper is breathed by the U.N. diplomats when terrorists deliberately target civilians. Israel is told to show restraint, while Hezbollah uses the U.N. zone of "protection" in southern Lebanon as cover to build a labyrinthine network of military facilities with impunity. At best this is incompetence; at worst it is a deliberate attempt to undermine the Israelis.

This same duplicity can be seen when it comes to the U.S. Many of the problems we see in Iraq can be traced to the U.N.'s refusal to support our invasion. The motive here can be traced to the Oil for Food Program. Two of the permanent Security Council members, France and Russia, appear to have had their votes bought on the subject of this war. Billions from this program were stolen and used by powerful people in those countries and the U.N. Saddam acted the way he did because he thought that the U.S. would not invade without the consent of the U.N. The dictator counted on his fountain of cash to discourage, and that's being nice, any move to overthrow his regime. Remember, the five permanent members of the Security Council can singlehandedly veto any move that comes before this body. It wasn't until the annual presidential speech in the fall of 2002 that Saddam realized that the U.S. would go without the approval of the U.N. That is when he began his clandestine removal of all of the incriminating evidence that he had accrued over the years. How different would the conflict in Iraq look today had a vast coalition taken on the task instead of a few allies?

As an American the globalists pose a very specific threat. They are looking to try to disarm our populace. They know that they could never rule this country so long as our people remain armed. Even if they were able to successfully infiltrate our government they know that our citizens would never accept their autocratic regime. Americans would rise up by the millions and defend our democracy by any means necessary. Internationalists are making attempts at trying to make the right to bear arms a notion of the past. The U.N. has already had conferences on such issues. Of course, they don't have names for these forums like "Let's disarm the civilians of the world," but their motives are easy to deduce. Armed American citizens are a significant barrier to their plans for world domination.

The E.U. shows many of the problems that come with globalism. Independent nations are forced by bureaucratic decree to adhere to policies that may not suit their country. Thus far, this has been mitigated by the fact that the E.U. is still more of a confederacy than a federation. Yet, we see the strong-arm tactics that this body has used on nations to meet the standards that the internationalists deem proper. Laws on abortion and gay rights have been contentious issues between this international body and member states, particularly in Eastern Europe. The E.U. has also made similar demands on nations seeking entry into their club, Turkey being the most obvious example. If we were to extrapolate from this model we have to have grave concerns for any involvement the U.S. may take in any international organization that is not completely voluntary.

The Constitution, and Declaration of Independence, of the United States of America makes no provision for any law higher than itself except that of our creator. No treaty or obligation supersedes these documents. I get chills down my spine when I hear Supreme Court justices citing foreign law in their opinions. I don't care what the "enlightened" jurists of the secular Western European nations do. Our own Constitution suffices for the law of the United States. We have developed a great system, despite all of its imperfections, and it is organically designed to fit the culture and nature of us as a people. Other countries can develop their own systems and we can all work together as separate nations.

One may be surprised but I don't want to withdraw from international organizations. I just want to review point by point where and how we decide to cooperate with other countries. America should remain a free and independent nation. We should also stay in these international bodies if only to help curb their tendencies toward one world government. The one real success that I have seen on the world stage of international cooperation is NATO. Yet, it is the nationally independent nature of this organization that I believe has allowed it to work. I also believe that the fact that all of the participating nations are democracies helps in the implementation of these varied countries' wills.

Globalism is a threat to all nations. It has the potential to create an all powerful international body that will ultimately become a dictatorship over all the countries of the world. We must resist the temptation to officially constitute all humanity into one body. For millennia nations and peoples have existed under their own power. Governments are the reflection of the growth of cultures over periods of time. Mankind functions best when we are allowed to keep to our respective and related interests. Each people has its way of life and manner of existence. To presuppose a bureaucracy of national elites onto all of the people of the world would be a dire mistake. Let us work together, let us seek solutions to global problems, but let us do so as free and independent countries working with the thought that we are all nation citizens of the planet Earth.

IT'S GEORGE BUSH'S FAULT!

It's George Bush's fault! The continual mantra of the left since the year 2000. Yes, no matter what it is, where it happened, or what time in history it took place, if it is bad, it's George Bush's fault. The divide between the left and the right is probably about as bad as it can get. And despite the fact that I am not a huge fan of good old George, no one can be as evil as the liberals think he is, and certainly no one can be so diabolically clandestine as they believe he is and as stupid as they think he is at the same time. I thought the right's hatred of Bill Clinton was bad, but it is nothing compared to the vitriol that the left directs at anything Bush. If he gave candy to children they would say that he was trying to give the kids diabetes so that the drug companies could make some more money off of them.

The left has gone so insane over the last seven years or so that they can't even think straight when it comes to the president. No matter what he does it is wrong. It doesn't matter if they supported the same idea yesterday; if George Bush suggests it the left is against it. This would be more comical if the stakes weren't so high. The liberals have taken their hatred of George Bush so seriously that they are willing to obstruct our national security to make him look bad. If he thinks that we need to fight in Iraq then they're against it. If he proposes personal accounts for Social Security then they're against it. If he proposes that they alter flight patterns to alleviate holiday travel headaches then they're against that too. It is irrelevant what he says; if it comes out of the mouth of George Bush then they are against it.

It has taken on the aura of a mental illness. There is nothing that this man can do that they would ever support. For years the Democrats whined that we had not sent enough troops to Iraq. Harry Reid, the Senate Majority

Leader, supported sending more troops until the moment that George Bush finally relented and agreed to do so. Then suddenly Mr. Reid flip-flopped positions and was against the extra troops. The Democrats are particularly intent on making sure that we lose the war in Iraq. They cannot tolerate a victory there because George Bush might actually get some of the credit. This is why they have done everything in their power to sabotage our war effort in Iraq. There is only one thing that they have not been willing to do, and that is the only thing that is actually in their power to do now that they control Congress. And that is to cut off funding for the war. Yet, they will never do that! That would be too obvious, that would be a step too far and they know that the American people would never tolerate that.

Yet, it doesn't stop with the war. No, apparently Bush even has power over nature. Have you ever heard of Hurricane Katrina? According to some on the left it too was Bush's fault. In fact, they even pointed to his refusal to sign the flawed Kyoto treaty as the cause of Katrina. It's irrelevant that hurricanes happen all the time. It's irrelevant that people had been warning of just such a disaster for decades. It's irrelevant that the levy commission spent more time on casinos than on the levies. It's irrelevant that Louisiana had an incompetent governor and New Orleans had an idiot for a mayor. Nope, none of that makes a difference; it was all George Bush's fault, and according to the vast intellect of Kanye West all help was delayed because George Bush hates black people. Not because the roads into Louisiana were covered with millions of trees, not because power lines were down, not because flood waters covered roadways or bridges were out, not because roving gangs were firing on rescue workers, not because the authorities of Louisiana did nothing to stop the looters. No, it was George Bush's hatred of black people that delayed the help. So again we can see how it was all Bush's fault.

It's amazing how much material the liberals' hatred of Bush can manufacture. The more I think about it the more I wonder if I should make it into a book by itself. I mean, one can take any issue, and if Bush has said something on the subject they are against it, and if he changed his mind they were sure to change theirs as well. Maybe Bush should come out against the war in Iraq. Maybe Bush should become pro-choice. Maybe he should say that he actually thinks that we should raise taxes. Possibly their mental illness is so strong it could even make them turn against their most sacred beliefs! Regardless of the issue all the conservatives would have to do is send George Bush out there to agree with the leftists' positions and they would have the liberals second guessing their every thought. I wonder if their hatred of George Bush is really that strong. It's worth a try, isn't it?

Remember, that according to the left Bush is an idiot. He also at the same time has been able, according to them, to engineer the evisceration of our constitutional rights without the government or courts being able to stop him. We all see the millions being rounded up and sent to concentration camps under the auspices of the Patriot Act. We have all seen the gulags teeming with the unjustly accused. We all know the knock on the door in the middle of the night means that the government is finally coming for you. Ask Rosie O'Donnell, ask Tim Robbins, ask Danny Glover, ask the Dixie Chicks, or the thousands of other entertainers who have voiced their opinions and faded away into the dark netherworld of the American reeducation camp system. America is under siege and it is all George Bush's fault.

On one hand it was George Bush that sacrificed the sympathy of the world after 9/11 for his plan to avenge his father with his war in Iraq. On the other it was George Bush who orchestrated the attacks on September 11th in the first place. It's not the increased demand by India and China that has driven up the cost of oil, but the shadowy hand of Bush trying to enrich his evil corporate friends. It's not the fanatical hatred of Islamist extremists that drive them to attack us, but the Bush invasion of Iraq and his failure to broker a peace agreement between the Palestinians and the

Israelis. It's not the tribal support given to Osama Bin Laden or the vast mountains of the Pakistan-Afghan border region that allow the most wanted man alive to remain at large. No, it is all George Bush's fault.

George Bush caused the Black Plague. George Bush started WWII. George Bush was actually the President of the Confederacy. He has a time machine and frequently uses it to go back and cause as much mischief as he can. Nothing is beyond this man, yet he is also a bumbling fool. Not one thing has ever gone wrong in history until he set foot on the stage as President of the United States. The world always loved us until January 2001. Nothing bad ever happened before that time. The world was a utopia and everything operated smoothly. Until George Bush arrived the Earth was a perfect place. Now we can look and see what this devilish imp has thrust upon the world, all the suffering that human beings have endured throughout all time and all places. When Buddha peeked his head over the palace walls it was George Bush he saw.

THE MEDIA

The media should not be an issue, but it has become one. Some studies have found that over thirty percent of journalists are self-described liberals and less than ten percent consider themselves conservative. This bias pollutes all of the information that we get. Outside of the Fox News channel, a few publications and newspapers, and talk radio, the news media in this country is extremely leftist. The partiality expressed is so pervasive that it is hardly noticed by the average person. We have seen the scandal at CBS with their use of false documents to try to harm the Bush reelection bid in 2004 and the use of Photoshop to enhance the appearance of damage to the city of Beirut in the Israeli-Hezbollah war of 2006. How many other attempts to alter the truth have not been revealed? The bias in the media is especially disconcerting because we need to understand the world around us in order to determine policies. When the stories we are being told do not accurately reflect what is occurring then we can not make informed decisions. When we cannot make informed decisions we cannot address events as they actually exist, and we may even make the wrong choices due to false or misleading information.

I have no problem with pundits or commentators who overtly state their bias. I have done so in the case of this book. What concerns me is the fact that the overwhelming majority of media publications present themselves as impartial when they are not. From CNN to *The New York Times* we can clearly deduce their bias. Their portrayal of the war in Iraq is one of the most obvious cases of their liberal leanings. When we were encountering the darkest days of the insurgency the war was the lead story on a daily basis. Now that things have taken a turn for the better the war has quickly become a non-story. The same can be said of the Abu Ghraib prisoner abuse scandal. Story after story was done in the attempt to exploit this failure of our military. Yet, we hardly ever hear about the grotesque atrocities of our terrorist enemies. In fact, some of the news organizations won't even call them terrorists. Abu Ghraib is a stain on America's image, and deservedly so, but we must not equivocate the actions of a few of our troops with the deliberate tactics of our enemies. Furthermore, we punished those involved at Abu Ghraib the terrorists revel in the torture and deaths of the innocent.

How many times have our strategies and tactics been publicized by the leftist media? Several incidents have occurred where the security of the U.S. was compromised by the actions of journalists. Both soldiers on the battlefield and citizens at home have been jeopardized by the media. They have revealed top secret programs that we used to get information on terrorists, published our plans for operations in the theatres of war, and continuously echo that our armed forces are stretched too thin. It almost seems at times that many on the left want the U.S. to lose the war. Their opposition to the war is their right, but when their actions facilitate the enemies' ability to prosecute the war, at what point does this become treason? Similar actions in WWII would have led to prison or worse for the perpetrators.

The daily presentation of the war in the media has been a great benefit to our enemies. Day in and day out we are shown the most gruesome images. These images are used as propaganda in the international media. The constant negativity only serves to heighten anti-American feelings and further distance us from the world as a whole. We need to have a balanced approach in the coverage of the war. Without such coverage public opinion is based on an erroneous construct that does not fit the realities on the ground. War is terrible, but is it necessary to gratuitously show every last drop of blood that is the result of this conflict? Could you imagine if the press had equivocated the brutality of our Nazi and Japanese enemies with the actions of American troops during WWII?

One example of media bias will help illuminate their leftist leanings. Since 2003 we have heard the daily repetition of how our intelligence failed in the lead-up to the Iraq war. The media continually trumpets the fact that we found no significant caches of weapons of mass destruction. I am not going to debate the veracity of this argument here, but I will point out that they have consistently repeated the mantra that our intelligence failed. Yet, when the National Intelligence Estimate in 2007 said that the Iranian nuclear program was effectively shelved a few years ago, everyone in the journalistic world jumped on the report. It was cited time and again to show that it was unnecessary to exert greater pressure on the Iranian regime. Suddenly, now that intelligence seemed to support the liberal agenda, its accuracy was unassailable and it was to be taken as gospel.

This bias is not only confined to the war. In fact it is just as pervasive on domestic issues. The most salient of these right now are the presidential elections and global climate change. The wives of the Republican candidates are fodder for all sorts of salacious accusations and comments, but the spouses of the Democrats are treated with kid gloves. Republicans are torn apart and vetted in every possible way and somehow it is off limits to mention the middle name of Mr. Obama or to juxtapose the myriad of positions that Queen Hillary has held on just about all issues. On global climate change, or global warming as the alarmists like to call it, we see the repeated attribution of this phenomenon to the emissions of CO_2 by mankind. The science is still unclear on this point. Yes, there is warming, there is climate change; but to assert that it is the result of our emission of this one gas is misleading at best. The liberals inculcate their mantras into the mind of the populace with their incessant repetitions of their bumper sticker slogans: "No blood for oil," "There were no weapons of mass destruction," "We attacked a country that did not attack us," "Pro-choice," "Polar bears are drowning," "Make love not war", and a thousand other phrases that are meant to evoke support for their causes. The left uses its preponderance of the control of the media to extol its values onto the masses.

One of the most telling moves by the liberals is their recent attempt to bring back the so-called Fairness Doctrine. This was a misguided concept that made the media strike a balance between various positions. When a liberal point of view was expounded a conservative point of view was supposed to be given an equal amount of time. The policy on its face may seem to be one that promotes balance, but it is little more than a hindrance of free speech. It was abandoned over twenty years ago. Yet, it is interesting to see a number of liberal lawmakers trying to revive this doctrine. They do not want to apply it to the media as a whole, but they only want to apply it to radio. I wonder why. Could it be that the left has near monolithic control of TV news and print journalism and is utterly unrepresented in talk radio? They have made their attempts to enter the realms of talk radio with Air America, but their efforts have fallen on deaf ears, or possibly the audiences just haven't liked what is being said. I would not be so suspicious if the Democrats wanted to apply the Fairness Doctrine across the board, but this is not their intent. Frankly, I don't want this doctrine applied anywhere. I will continue to rely on the market to determine what media people choose, even if I feel that the current situation greatly favors my adversaries. If my ideas are worthy then others will listen.

I know that I see the media through the colors of my own perceptions. Yet, it is abundantly clear that the left does everything in its power to control the flow of information getting to the American public. This is becoming increasingly difficult with the rise of alternative sources for our news and opinion. First it was talk radio, then came the likes of the Fox News network, and most recently the explosion of media on the internet. I'm not suggesting that all of the information on the internet is accurate—quite the contrary, this is one of its biggest impediments– but that we no longer have to depend on the established sources of the media. It is no surprise that the major networks' nightly newscasts are losing viewers. I feel that almost every word they speak is meant to advance their liberal agenda.

The most recent wave of propaganda has surrounded the environmental movement. We see countless articles and stories done on so-called "green" issues. Time and again we hear the jargon of the anti-capitalist, anti-Western, radical environmentalists spewed as if it were fact. Stories about famine in Africa are implicitly laid at the door of the greedy Westerner. Polar bears are shown adrift on a single sheet of ice in a vast sea. Companies are made to look as if they are indifferent to the environmental impact that they have and are blamed for all of the ecological problems in the world. Yet, they consistently portray the consumer, that is me and you, as if we are some sort of champion if we don't use a plastic bag or if we buy a more energy-efficient appliance. I do not decry efforts to reduce our impact on the globe, but only that we have less of a heroic tone when it comes to individuals and a less antagonistic approach toward business. We cannot "save the Earth." We can only stop ruining it for humans and our other neighbors.

The debate over many issues exemplifies the media's bias. When the SCHP program was debated in Congress the press and news outlets consistently tried to frame the positions of the Republicans as if they were trying to take healthcare away from children. This ignored the fact that they wanted to increase the program, but did not want it to expand to where it would become the first step in socialized medicine in this country. It also ignored the fact that many people in this program were neither children nor poor. The same leftist tilt is used in discussing the federal budget. We see the tax cuts getting the blame for our soaring deficits, not the fact that the government is overspending. I actually recall seeing a pundit on a panel on CNN act surprised when he heard the statement that tax cuts increase revenue to the federal government. He was either disingenuous or had no business being on a show that discusses political and economic topics.

We have to carefully observe how the media characterizes specific people and stories. They can have an enormous impact on the psyche of the nation. The repetition of slogans and mantras can infect the mind. How vital was Josef Goebbels in the creation of the Holocaust? How important is the use of propaganda in the dehumanization of another person? I do not think our current media has crossed into this territory, but I do believe that they use a much more gradual, steady approach in their attempt to push their agenda forward. Every form of media is being used to inculcate the ideology of the left into daily life. If they were so confident of the viability of their ideas why do they feel so impelled to silence the voices of the conservatives? I have no fear of their opinions, I simply disagree with them. I wish to make no moves to silence their voice when will they stop trying to drown ours out?

EDUCATION

I have so much to say on this issue that it is hard to even know where to begin. I have spent a great portion of my life in the schools, first as a student in the public school system, then as a student in college, then as a teacher, and as a student again in a post-graduate program. Some of my experiences have been good and others have been excruciatingly painful. The education system in this country is abysmal. Our students are falling behind the rest of the industrialized nations of the world. We have to overhaul our system from top to bottom. Many of the problems we have in our schools can be traced back to the failed policies and influence of the liberals. I am currently in my eleventh school year of teaching. I worked briefly in the public schools and have been fortunate enough to find a home in a very unique Special Education high school. Teaching is by far the toughest job I have ever had, and by far the best job that I have ever had.

The foremost point that I want to make is that money is not the problem. The U.S. currently spends more per student than almost any other nation. In fact, many of the regions of this country that spend the highest amount of dollars on average per student have some of the worst results. The problems can be found mostly in bureaucracy, lack of discipline, tedious standardization, the teaching of unnecessary material, and the meddling of politicians. The education system can be fixed, but it is not the job of the federal government. The best thing they can do is get the hell out of the classroom. We also need to get the litigious and feminizing left out of our schools as well.

Our schools seem to have come to think that self-esteem is more important than correct answers. Somehow self-pride has come to replace actual knowledge. We too often see that professionals are more concerned with how their students feel than with what they are actually learning. America produced some of the greatest minds that we ever did when we had a system based on merit. Now we have a system collapsing in on itself and it is because it is more concerned with everything other than the students learning. We must return to the day when school was about academic education. Trust me, I understand the importance of the students' personal perception of themselves, but not knowing how to read or how to count the correct change one should get can be just as devastating to their self-esteem. We need again to have students who have mastered the basics before we teach extraneous subject matter.

One of the most important problems in school derives from this notion the liberals have that self-actualization should be the foremost thing taught in our schools. This has led to an underlying narcissism being inculcated into our students. Many walk away with the idea that their happiness is the most important thing in the world. They have been taught that so long as they are smiling all is right in the universe. This is part of the reason that so few Americans truly understand the world beyond our shores. It is also the reason that so many are caught up in the emptiness of our popular culture. True education comes with learning the fundamentals first, and then moving on to a broader understanding of all of the facets of one's own culture, and then to an understanding of the world as a whole. I don't care how good an idiot feels about oneself, that person is still an idiot. Ignorance is not a substitute for actual comprehension. The truly educated individual has a grasp on all of the varying disciplines that make up our world, and they also should have a rudimentary understanding of the other cultures that make up the human race.

One of the basic notions so detrimental to the education of American students is the idea that it is bad to fail. I never had this idea illuminated to me more than when I was studying to get my Special Education

Certification in college. One incident should suffice to exemplify this point. In one of my classes the professor was talking about what to do when marking assessments (otherwise known as tests). The instructor went on about how we should not use red to mark answers incorrect, but that we should use other colors. She went into a diatribe about how red signified failure to the students and how it made them feel bad about themselves. I raised my hand and asked if I could comment on the matter. I asked the professor if it wasn't the point in marking the answer wrong to signify that the student had failed to adequately respond to the question. I said that this was the whole reason I marked the assessments in the first place. This way the students could learn what they did right and what they did wrong, thus giving them a basis from which to improve. Furthermore, I said that if we followed her logic how many years would it be until some other professor was now teaching that red should be used to mark tests now because all other colors signify failure to the students and it makes them feel bad about themselves? Needless to say, she said very little in response.

Part of life is failing. Part of life is not only finding out what you are good at, but what you are not so good at. Our education system has become almost devoid of this notion. We have schools that do not use grades, gym classes that are prohibited from playing dodge ball, and rewards that have no merit. All of these practices are intertwined. They emanate from educators who are immersed in the doctrines of the left. They believe that grades don't have any meaning except to show who has performed the best according to the teacher's parameters. They think that dodge ball creates a hierarchy based on strength and athletic prowess. They feel it necessary to create rewards for doing what should be done in the first place. All this is absolute garbage! Grades are a reflection of what the teacher has taught in class. The smart student who isn't athletic realizes that the best way to handle dodge ball is to get out of the game as quickly as possible. The really smart students try to get one of their friends to hit them with the ball before the big angry jock does it. And any person who has the simplest understanding of life knows when they are being given an award that has no meaning. Education must be returned to the realm of academics and away from building self-esteem through false pretenses.

Another salient problem in our schools is discipline. What happened to the time when a single nun with a ruler could control a class of fifty kids? What happened to the time when if a student got in trouble at school they got in trouble at home as well? I remember being in the public school and making a call home to tell a sixth grader's parent why she would have detention the next day. I was shocked when the parent said to me after I explained what had happened in class that, "That's not how she tells it!" I was stunned. I simply politely informed her that I was telling the truth and that I had nothing against her daughter. I also reminded her that an eleven-year-old might go a long way in stretching the truth in order to avoid punishment.

I can't tell you how many times students have tried to threaten me, both legally and physically. I have always handled the situation the same way. When it has been a legal threat I have told them to talk to their parents and go get a lawyer, I'd be happy to defend myself in the court of law. Oddly enough, not one student has ever taken me up on the offer. When it has been a physical threat I have gently reminded them of the fact that if they lay one hand on me it is my right to defend myself by all means necessary. Here too, I've never had a problem get beyond me having to toss a table and grab a chair. Mind you, I have worked for ten years with the emotionally disturbed and sometimes we have to deal with truly threatening physical confrontations. It is certainly not a job for the faint of heart.

Schools cannot function effectively when the staff is prevented from exercising discipline. The students should not be allowed to run the school. Yet, we see the petty logic-twisting lawsuits filed by the likes of the ACLU inhibiting the professionals from controlling what happens in their community and the classrooms. Teachers should not be held to an artificially high standard of behavior. They should not be expected to bear egregious insults and not respond at all. Yes, I understand the role of professional decorum, but we are human beings as well. The more students feel that they have the right to act in the most offensive and rude manners possible the more they will do so. We need to reestablish the notion that it is the staff that has the power in the school, not the students. Parents must also realize that their baby may not always comport themselves in such a positive way when they are not present. When the professionals get out of hand there is plenty of recourse to deal with their behavior; we must stop the processes that have made the staff guilty until proven innocent. All this mentality does is to foster an environment in which students feel that they have the power to control the day-to-day business that occurs in the school. It becomes impossible to teach when the instructor is forced to explain every requirement in a class and every direction that is given to their students.

The fear of legal problems also limits the effectiveness of how our education system is run. Obviously there needs to be the ability of parents and students to protect themselves from untoward acts by professionals. Yet, we see the threat of lawsuits eroding the ability of educators to do the job of educating. The public schools are especially fearful of legal action. Counselors and teachers are wary of addressing problems that they see might be developing; instead they wait until the problems actually manifest themselves and then it is too late. This particularly applies to students gravitating towards gangs and criminal behaviors, risky sexual activity, and drugs and alcohol. Staff members are dissuaded from speaking to students about these problems by administrators because they feel preventative action may expose the school system to lawsuits. We pay professionals to utilize their skills; part of those abilities are their intuitive understanding of young people.

We must provide a basis by which staff can perform to their highest potential.

As I have said, I teach in a school for the emotionally disturbed and those with learning and behavioral disabilities. Thank God the school is private! Yet, we still have contact with the public schools because it is the districts that send students to my school when they have been unable to deal with the child or young adult. Despite a lack of discipline in the public schools what they do address they often address in an inordinate manner. This especially applies to no tolerance policies. I have had students sent to my school, which costs about four to five times what it costs the districts per student, for one incident. Usually it is a fight or the possession of drugs and alcohol. Many of these students should have had the chance to remain in their school or at least a chance to work their way back, but too often a particular educator, counselor, or administrator simply dislikes the student so much that this never happens. Students in my school will typically receive a half-hour detention at lunch for offenses for which a district would suspend a student. A little bit of patience and tolerance could go a long way in increasing the time that students spend in the classroom and possibly keep more students in their districts.

One of the other advantages of teaching in a private school is that I have a greater leeway in how I meet the curriculum standards. The main academic subjects that I teach are history and environmental science. Many of the documentaries and movies that I show in classes would not be permitted in the public schools, particularly those I have about WWII. Many would be deemed to be too graphic in the public school setting. Administrators would be worried that parents might call in because their child was upset by the brutality of war. Before I show any of these videos I always give the students the choice of an alternative assignment or the permission to step out of the classroom if the need should arise.

Yet, I believe it is because the public schools refuse to show the realities of history that so many Westerners have no concept of what war is. Too many people think that the war in Iraq is a major conflict. Though it is costly to those who are involved it is small compared to WWII or even Vietnam. It would take sixty years at this rate for us to match the death toll in Iraq with that of Vietnam. Another example is the fact that so many people believe that the U.S. was wrong to drop the atom bombs on Hiroshima and Nagasaki. Few of my students walk out of my class with that notion. They have seen the brutality of the Japanese Imperial Army in Nanking and the smoldering piles of charred bodies of the soldiers who chose a suicidal Banzai charge over surrender. They have read the diary writings of those held in the concentration camps and heard the stories of the ritual beheadings of downed American pilots in the Pacific. I don't use this material to be gratuitous, but to display the horrible ferociousness of war. When people know the truth it becomes absurd to make comparisons between America and the Nazis or Hitler and George Bush.

We need to establish a system that is based on accomplishment. Students should not get social promotions to the next grade. When a student has not mastered the skills at one level they should not be moved ahead to the next. They should also not be inundated with extraneous materials like diversity appreciation or *Heather has Two Mommies*. It is the parents' job to teach specific morals and values. The schools need to teach academics and the generalities of what makes a good citizen in a democracy. Too often we see liberal and socialist values being passed on to our students as if they are facts. The same can be said of scientific theories that are presented to make the universe appear to be nothing more than a series of inevitable chance occurrences. These tangential materials can be saved for those students who have attained the basic academic standards.

This leads me to another point. I feel that the accent on Special Education for students with special needs is good, but should we not put the same amount of time, money, and effort into educating the gifted? Why are there so few schools for those who excel? As much as it benefits the society as a whole to assist those who do not perform well, how much greater would it benefit society to give special attention into nurturing the talents of the gifted? I fear that we are allowing the exceptional abilities of too many students to remain untapped. We need bright minds to engineer the future and advance our cultural pursuits. America is falling behind in the intellectual fields of the world. We cannot maintain our standard of living if we do not produce the minds that will shape the future.

Most recent efforts to improve our education system have been based on meeting arbitrary benchmarks and passing standardized tests. These efforts have also been primarily the brain children of politicians. Their lack of understanding of what causes problems in schools reflects strongly in their erroneous solutions to the ailments that plague our system. Let's take a look at the No Child Left Behind Act. This was a bipartisan effort of Congress to address our failing education system. All it did was increase the certification standards for educators and make it necessary for students to pass a new standardized test. First of all, the problems in the schools are not because teachers don't know the subject matter or don't know how to teach. Students aren't learning because of a myriad of problems outside the schools in their homes and our culture. Teachers do not need to have a degree in a subject in order to teach a subject; this is especially true at the elementary level. Standardized tests are also one of the worst assessment tools. I have had the luxury of reading these tests aloud to students that have this modification in their education plan. These tests are confusing, misleading, and even downright inaccurate. They in no way show what a student knows, but only if they know what has been put on the test. The last thing our education system needs is to have educators teaching to a standardized test. Solutions to our schools problems need to come from educators, not politicians.

We also see the creeping hand of liberalism when it comes to textbooks. Most companies will not publish materials that cannot be used in California due to its large population. Yet, the stipulations that California puts into the requirements are not only leftist, but they often approach the brink of insanity. So many ludicrous proposals are made in the state that it is often hard to know which ones have become standards and which ones have not. I have heard that the state wanted to limit stereotypes from their texts. In order to do this each race, gender, and creed had limitations on how they could be portrayed in schoolbooks. Jews couldn't be lawyers and Asians couldn't be doctors and so on and so forth. Recently I have heard there is an attempt to make teachers stop using the word parent in schools. This is some pitiful idea no doubt proposed by some bleeding heart to protect the fragile psyche of some kid without a parent. All these ridiculous notions do is inoculate students from the real world, and it will only be that much harder for them to deal with the real world when they enter it.

Some proposals to improve the schools center on teachers. One of these is the idea that teachers should be assessed on the performance of their students. Without an elaborate system to objectify how this would be measured this idea will not work. First we must look at the plethora of variables that each student brings into the classroom. How will dysfunctional home lives, learning disabilities, and behavioral problems be factored into my class' performance. One persistently disruptive student could diminish the outcome of an entire class. This is part of the reason that I don't think we can compare the public and private schools. Private schools choose who they admit and can dismiss a student at anytime for almost any reason. Public schools have to take every student who lives in a district. They are forced to maintain troubled students for as long as possible due to the Least Restrictive Environment requirement imposed by federal law. Assessing teachers on the performance of a class made up from students who can have a wide variety of strengths and weaknesses is unfair. This idea might be more tenable if educators were permitted to pick their students. How can we compare the effectiveness of one teacher to another if the abilities from one class to the next can be so disparate?

Frequently we hear the idea of vouchers bandied about. In a few places it has been tried with a modicum of success. I have to admit I am a bit ambivalent about the notion. On one hand I do see the right of parents to choose where they spend their tax money. On the other hand I do see how this could lead to two different sets of schools, one where all the students are given a good education and the other that will have all of the failing students. I feel that this idea would probably be best tried out if it was done on a local and regional basis rather than all across the nation. Each locality could investigate whether vouchers can improve their system and how they would implement it if they wanted to give it a try. At this point we must be willing to utilize more radical ideas in attempting to remedy our failing education system.

One thought I rarely hear being discussed on this issue is the ridiculous amount of paperwork that is required of teachers. Teachers spend about as much time on tedious and redundant paperwork as they do on teaching. I'm not talking about grading work, but forms and reports that the state or federal government have mandated. Writing lesson plans every year for the same class is a waste of my time. Reading outdated files that tell me how a high school student performed in the first grade does not improve my classroom performance. A recent New Jersey law has made it necessary for the professionals to calculate what students are buying from the school for breakfast and lunch and submit it to the state. That sounds like a good use of an educator's time. The bureaucratic red tape in the education system does nothing to benefit our children and only serves to take time away from the teacher's preparation for the classroom.

Often I hear people say, or read in editorials, that teachers are overpaid. This is a joke! The only professional class of people that get less than educators do is nurses. I am getting paid in my eleventh year of teaching what a computer programmer might start at in a company. I am not arguing for higher salaries, just the recognition that educators be recompensed fairly. Remember, we are teaching the most valuable resource our nation has: its children. My day does not end when the bell rings at the end of school. Much of my planning, grading, and preparation are done at home. Also the constant honing of my skills and knowledge base is an ongoing process.

Thus far I have concentrated on elementary and high school education. I think it is necessary to take a look at higher education. The colleges and universities are bastions of the liberals. They, for the most part, have become factories for socialist and secular ideologies. Professors can hold the most radically leftist ideals and remain in their positions with impunity. They often promote their belief systems and belittle those with whom they disagree. Students are penalized when they defend or articulate positions that the left do not hold. Students who are conservative are often forced to make the choice between silence or expressing their views and having their grades suffer. Right-leaning orators have been shouted down at universities, such as Columbia in New York City, and self-professed America haters hold sway at most of our institutions of higher learning. I have no problem with academic freedom so long as it is applied to all.

My own personal experience in the halls of higher education was not so different. Except for a few outstanding professors I had, most were just parrots of the left. The typical professor held a world view that saw America as an evil empire and Western culture as a whole as corrupt. Their idea of diversity was to blame all things on white males and they were tolerant of all religions except Christianity and sometimes Judaism. The constant harping on race, gender, and ethnicity did more to divide the students than it did to bring them together. Many fellow students came to identify who they were with what they were. Is not

America supposed to be based on the idea that what makes us a person comes from the content of our character? I'm pretty sure a very gifted orator and preacher said something to that effect several decades ago.

College classes often became a parlor game of what group could claim to be the most oppressed. Victimization was a disease that everybody had, except white Christian males. If it were not for the oppressive imperialist white man all other groups would not be so held back from their rightful place in our society. I must admit that I was almost sucked into this vacuum of liberalism as well. The constant repetitions of these notions crept into my way of thinking. The only period of doubt I have ever had about my religious faith was for a sixth-month period right after I started college. My belief in the strengths of America was also almost overridden with the persistent focus on all of our faults and past injustices. Rarely were the accomplishments and ever-increasing freedom of our country mentioned. I always point out in my classes that only a very few people were allowed to vote when our Constitution went into effect. I also point out that slavery, the second-class citizenship of women, and a myriad of other odious impositions existed in our society at that time. Yet, look at us today: We certainly are not perfect, but for the most part people of all races, sex, ethnicity, and creeds are able to fully exploit the opportunities our society presents on their own personal merits.

Much needs to be done to remedy the overall academic climate in this country. From pre-school to the university we have innumerable problems. We spend too much money for poor results. We have schools overrun by out-of-control students. Politicians continually try to address the situation with draconian regulations and paperwork. Standardized tests have a role in education, but they are not the barometer of achievement that their proponents believe them to be. We are trying so hard to work with those on the low end of the academic scale that we are neglecting those on the higher end. Again and again money is thrown at our educational institutions in the vain hope that somehow this time it will correct the deficiencies in our school system.

In essence we need in some ways to look behind, to look at what worked in the past. Grading based on performance not feeling, allowing for educators to establish a climate of control in their classroom and an atmosphere that permits for learning, teaching about the strengths of our culture and not only its faults. We have a vast resource of intellectual potential in our three hundred million people; it is finally the time to recapture this asset. Our technology and production helped win WWII. America put the first man on the moon and our republic helped lay the foundation for democracies all around the globe. Let us not fail in our efforts to pass this greatness onto the next generations.

CRIME AND PUNISHMENT

I hope Dostoyevsky can forgive me for using the title of his most excellent book, but it's just too appropriate. I have the suspicion that many who consider themselves conservatives may not be too happy with all of my suggestions in this chapter. That will simply be their failure to accept my thoughts on this issue for the purpose that I intend, which is simply to end the cycle of incarceration and crime. Though I do believe that the punishment should fit the crime I also believe that the purpose of our penal system should be to rehabilitate those we can. In some ways my career as a teacher of those who have behavioral problems has given me some extra insight into how our judicial and prison systems deal with those who have gone astray of the law. Too often I have seen juveniles that have made a mistake be captured by the clutches of professional criminals and fall into a life of crime as well. Our current methods of dealing with crime tend often to have the result of causing more crime. This applies to our prisons as well as our courts. America has one of the highest incarceration rates in the world. Yet, we have a significant recidivism rate and little is done to address these individuals before they find themselves in the hands of the authorities.

I'm not making a plea to have pity on the poor criminal. If I were to do that I would be a liberal. Rather, I hope to look into the mechanisms that might make our system more efficient and less conducive to the creation of greater criminality. In order to do this we need to investigate our laws, punishment, and methods of incarceration. We also have to look at what situations in society tend to produce anti-social behaviors and how this can be addressed before people become adjudicated. Too often we throw individuals into jail for infractions that do not warrant this punishment. Our system also permits for a climate in the prisons that foster increased criminal behavior. What can be done to reduce the size of our inmate population and what can be done to create an atmosphere in prisons that does not lead to more deviancy is crucial to addressing this problem?

In this case I will address this topic from the most critical problems backward to its sources. Simply put, our prisons usually make prisoners worse. How can we expect anyone to be truly rehabilitated while facing violent crimes, gangs, and a culture that at best encourages and rewards skirting the rules? Jail needs to be unpleasant, but it shouldn't be hell. Throwing people into the depths of society will rarely yield good results. We need to create a culture that protects the inmates, both physically and socially, while at the same time having their experience be a part of the restitution that they are making to those that they have wronged. Incarceration should be designed to make as many people as possible in the system able to return as productive members of our society. To do anything less is to only facilitate a revolving door that continually returns the criminals to the institutions that are supposed to rehabilitate them.

To address these problems we must first look at the prisons themselves. The current system of incarceration does not do enough to keep the violent criminals away from those who have committed non-violent crimes. In far too many cases these prisoners are allowed to mix. I suggest that the best way to eliminate many of the problems we see being caused in our jails is to stratify the population. Prisons should work on a tiered system where those of comparable crimes are housed together. In this way the interaction between varying degrees of criminals would be mitigated. If financially feasible, I would also propose the possibility of isolating as many prisoners as possible. Thieves should not have murderers breathing down their necks and petty criminals should not have to worry about a shower with a brutal rapist. The intermingling of the prison population also heightens the potential for gang activity to influence those who find themselves in our system. Many on the outside do not realize the pressures that are exerted on those who need protection inside the jails. They also do not realize how effectively the need for protection within the system can be manipulated to get prisoners to do things that they might not have done, had they not been faced with such situations.

I have seen many of my former students enter the system as wannabes and come out of it hardened criminals with gang affiliations. I have also seen vulnerable students manipulated by gangs into doing their bidding. To break this cycle we must destroy the gang-producing factories that the jails and streets have become. What I offer here are only suggestions that those who directly deal with crime and punishment must refine and turn into reality. It is easy to turn a blind eye to what individuals will do when faced with issues of survival, but to do this is to ignore the underlying causes of what leads people into organized crime. Prisons are being used as a production line for gang members. They also are being used to refine and hone the brutality and obedience of these new recruits.

Too many citizens in this country do not comprehend the correlation between prisons, gang activity, and a significant amount of the crime being committed on the outside. Too many people also only see gangs as a problem for inner-city minority groups. This could not be further from the truth. Many average Americans do not recognize how many seemingly pointless or random crimes are actually the result of gang initiations and retaliation. In order to weaken the power of these organizations we must disrupt the culture that they are using to foster their goals. Again, I will admit that I don't have all of the answers, but we must change our methods of incarceration if we ever want rehabilitation to be a reality for most prisoners. Strictly limiting the interaction in the prisons would be one of the best places to start. It is also imperative that we address the need to remove problem inmates from the general population. We also must take a look at expanding the definition of exactly what does constitute a problem inmate. The system needs to stop tolerating the promotion of gang culture. Most of these prisoners are decorated with tattoos that explicitly express their positions in these organizations. Due to the extreme detriment that these cultures cause to the society as a whole, I believe we need to address this problem much more vigorously. Divide and conquer must become a standard mantra within the American prison system. I realize that cost will be a prohibitive possibility in any changes we may make, but we must do all that we can within these constraints.

Beyond dealing with the negative aspects of our penal system we must establish a positive alternative. Prisons can offer more than just punishment. Many of the root causes of criminal behavior are due to poor education, abuse, neglect, and a lack of opportunity. In order to mitigate these circumstances our prisons need to better utilize the time that inmates spend while incarcerated. Most of these problems are already given attention, but improving and innovating these programs is necessary to rehabilitation. Providing inmates with an education permits for greater opportunity once they reenter society. Helping inmates cope with the social traumas that they may have endured in life will also lead to the release of more stable and functional individuals to the outside world as a whole. Removing people from society for a period of time does little if we do not try to address what has created the person that they have become. Many will never change, but it is a disservice to us all if we fail to even try to make those changes happen.

Therapy, education, and job training can go a long way in rehabilitating prisoners. The efforts that we put into these programs will be returned by their results. We cannot continue to treat imprisonment as only a punishment. Many of those who are in the system need to have problems addressed if they are to ever have a hope at becoming productive members of our society. As the institutions of our penal institutions exist today we are accomplishing little in the tangible reformation of our inmate population. The cost to society is incalculable in terms of money, emotional pain, and time. Recidivism needs to be reduced if we are ever to get a grip on the problems of criminality. This can only happen when we treat the causes of anti-social behavior. This can only be accomplished by providing intensive behavior modification and imparting skills that will benefit the life of an inmate once they are back into the daily routines of society. For those who are incorrigible we need to lock them away for as long as possible.

We also need to consider those methods of dealing with criminals that fall short of institutionalized prisons. Boot camps, community service, and other innovative programs need to be utilized and explored to diminish the numbers of people in our judicial system. Crimes of a lesser nature need to be dealt with in less restrictive manners than we are currently doing so. Minor offenses do not warrant the full weight of our penal system. The best methods for dealing with infractions of the law that are not serious, or repeated, are fines, community service, and non-residential programs. Far too many people are spending time in our prisons who do not belong there. To reduce costs and concentrate our efforts on those who belong in jail we must change the way in which we deal with minor crimes.

Reducing costs also can be approached in two other ways. One is to get rid of all non-essential amenities in the prisons. The other is to utilize inmates in productive labor that maintains the jails or creates products. Why should those who are incarcerated be given free, and better, healthcare than law-abiding citizens? Why should those in jail have access to top of the line technologies like televisions and computers free of charge? How come some inmates are receiving food that is of higher quality than many on the outside can afford? I'm not saying that these things need to be eliminated altogether, just that those who are in prison should have to earn privileges like these. One prisoner recently sued because he was being denied a sex change operation at taxpayers' expense. Our penal system has to stop being a vacation spa for the legally challenged. It also has to stop being a place where people who are supposed to be getting punishment and rehabilitation live in the lap of luxury.

Prisons need to start to use the vast pool of labor that inmates can provide to reduce costs, provide public works, and generate cash. Prisoners are already utilized in many of these ways, but we need to expand these programs as much as possible. The jails must use prisoners for any job that they can be used for within the walls of the institution, from filing non-sensitive paperwork to maintenance. We should also look to use the inmates to produce some of their own food in gardens. This will have the added benefit of showing those involved the value of working the land and the rewards that come with it. I would even suggest that where it is possible animal husbandry should be an addition to such programs. Working with the natural world does wonders for people, especially those with troubled souls. Public works projects can also provide many of the same benefits and reduce tax expenditures at the same time. Finally, we could use prisons to produce goods that will offset the financial burden of their incarceration. All of these ideas need to be further delineated by the institutions and communities that would be involved.

One of the more salient issues concerning our penal system is the death penalty. I am not opposed to the death penalty in principle, but I am very wary of allowing it to be used easily. Obviously, the danger of using it on the innocent is a paramount concern. We also need to look at the high cost that comes with litigating this punishment into a reality. My home state of New Jersey just committed the egregious offense of eliminating the death penalty altogether despite the fact that the majority of its citizens wanted it to remain a legal option. I don't care if the death penalty is a deterrent or not. I view it as a punishment and nothing else. When the guilt of an individual is beyond question it is the right of society to administer this most severe penalty. When its cost is prohibitive or any possibility of innocence remains then I think it is best to refrain from this form of punishment. When this is the case true life in prison should suffice in lieu of the death penalty.

Aside from changing our systems of punishment and rehabilitation we need to focus on preventing people from turning to a life of crime. I work in a school that has students that are at risk for doing just that. What my experience has taught me is that it is very hard to combat these anti-social behaviors. Part of the problem is that the school day is short, only five days a week, and closed for two months during the summer. What I extol to my students during the day is attacked by bad influences and examples once they return to their lives at home from those they associate with and the society as a whole. I have also come to realize that intelligence does not directly correspond to how people act in their lives. Some of the brightest students I have ever had are incarcerated as I write. What I do know is that it takes consistent and persistent effort from those involved with a young person to make a change in their behavior possible, and a fundamental realization from that individual that the path that they are following has no positive outcomes. Until someone grasps the concept and realities that their choices will yield only unwanted consequences, no real epiphany on their part is possible. We can help from the outside, but real transformation comes from within.

As a society we need to put as much effort as possible into providing realistic and viable alternatives to our youth if we want to deter criminal behavior. Supporting families, reducing the allure of gangs, and providing effective education are some of the most basic steps that we can take. Crime and punishment in our society is expensive financially and socially. Changing some of the fundamental approaches we have to these problems is essential to more effectively dealing with the criminal culture that has evolved within our society. Continuing to use the same old failed approaches to crime and punishment will only yield the same old failed results that we have gotten over the last several decades.

LITIGATION

Few activities do as much to damage our nation as litigation. The cost and inhibitions that unnecessary lawsuits bring to our culture are incalculable. How much time, money, and effort are squandered away on trying to ensure our legal safety? There is no recessed corner of our society that is protected from the extended arms of the greedy lawyers. Just stop and think for a moment about how many events and circumstances in our lives are the results of litigious attempts to make money from a minor inconvenience or error. How many cases in the courts boggle the mind and make us question the very sanity of our system? Jesus said it best when he said if you meet your adversary on the road to the courthouse (obviously I'm paraphrasing) you would do best to settle your differences right there rather than bring it before the magistrates.

Clearly, litigation has its place, but how much are we hindered by the whimsical uses of our court systems? The British do not seem to have as many frivolous court cases as we have here in America. This is probably due to the fact that if the plaintiff loses they have to pay the legal fees of the defendant. I don't know if we need to go that far in the U.S., but we certainly do need to change our system as a whole. The high cost of healthcare is directly tied to the malpractice insurance that doctors must have in order to protect themselves from lawsuits. Yes, we need a method to address negligent care from physicians, but the exorbitant compensation from lawsuits is causing the high costs of healthcare. This same effect can be seen in many other facets of our society as well. There is not a business, institution, or organization that does not suffer from the incurred costs of lawsuits or the prospect of preventing them.

Think about your daily life. From the simplest coffee cup to the constant disclaimers run in every ad and television show, we see the effect of potential legal action. When I pick up a paper cup at work that is specifically designed to hold hot liquids, is it necessary to have the cup have a warning that says, "Caution: Contents may be hot"? If somebody is so stupid as to not realize this don't they deserve to get burned? I am tired of having our society reduced to the lowest common denominator. The cost to our country not only comes in monetary value, but in a waste of resources and time.

Let's take a brief look at the infamous coffee case. If my memory serves me right, this case was twofold. The first part took place when McDonald's was found liable for a burn a customer received from its coffee. In the first case the company was warned that it maintained the temperature at a level that could cause third degree burns. Part of the settlement was that they would lower the temperature of the coffee so it could not induce these severe injuries. Apparently McDonald's did not fully comply with this ruling. When a second customer was burned— mind you, she had the hot coffee between her legs—she sued and also won, but this time punitive damages were added to the compensatory damages. Now the company had to pay a million dollars for this incident. I understand the concept behind the punitive reward, but this is applied almost across the board. Companies settle most lawsuits to defer the costs of litigation and possible exorbitant damages. Every purchase we make has a fraction of these payments attached.

One of the favorite targets of the lawyers has been the tobacco industry. In some cases the payouts have been in the hundreds of billions. These damages were rewarded to those who were sickened by smoking and to the survivors that were left behind from those who died from the habit. I could see if these cases were events of the time before 1970, when the dangers of smoking were not quite as widely known as they are today. But these people have no excuse: they lit up knowing the dangers. How is this the tobacco companies' fault? How are they liable for the conscious decision by people to smoke? I feel bad about their illnesses and the loss of their loved ones, but they made the choice to smoke. I say this as a smoker.

We have also seen a number of cities try to sue gun manufacturers for the use of illegal guns on their streets. Yes, I will repeat that again, a number of cities are trying to sue gun manufacturers for the use of illegal guns on their streets. Maybe it's just me, but how is a company liable for the illegal use of its product? Should car manufacturers be liable when someone deliberately runs down another individual with their car? Should bathtub and shower companies be sued when someone slips in the tub? Where does it end? By this reasoning we can construct an infinite series of events that would confer liability on any company or person for just about anything. Lawsuits were designed to punish negligence or criminal indifference, not to be a lottery for the ignorant and greedy.

Criminals who have been intent on robbing businesses, homes, and institutions have been injured in their illicit pursuits and sued their victims. In some of the more outlandish cases they have won. Falling through a skylight, tripping on a roller skate on the stairs, and other mishaps by criminals has been used to reward their illegal behavior. We need to allow judges greater leeway in throwing out these frivolous lawsuits. When one is engaged in the commission of an illegal act they throw away all their rights. Allowing them to sue their intended victims is truly criminal.

One incident that illuminates this point brilliantly is the case of the great shootout in Southern California several years ago. Those who have not heard about it simply need to know that two men wearing body armor and heavily armed with automatic weapons got into an intense exchange of gunfire with law enforcement. I don't remember if they actually pulled off their robbery, but that is irrelevant. These two men opened fire on the city streets, shot at civilians and law enforcement personnel deliberately, and showed no mercy to those they had attacked. The battle raged and there was little that could be done because the authorities were out-gunned and had little ability to pierce their body armor defenses. One culprit either killed himself on purpose or by accident and the other was finally wounded and surrendered. The latter died from a loss of blood while law enforcement tried to ensure that the area was secure enough to bring in paramedics. His family is suing! What a travesty of justice. This piece of garbage kills and wounds people creating the conditions that lead to his death, and his relatives are suing on his behalf. The fact that the case is even being given consideration is an insult to all the victims and people who had their lives destroyed or put into danger by his actions.

Some other cases that exemplify the failings of our legal system aren't quite so serious. How about the judge who sued a dry cleaner for fifty million dollars for losing his "favorite" pair of pants? This idiot actually had the audacity to sit in the courtroom crying over his pants in a pathetic attempt to establish damages based on mental anguish. Thus far, he has not gotten what he wants and may even have to pay the legal fees of the couple that owned the business, but they still had to endure the time and energy given to this absurdity. They had even offered him thousands of dollars in lieu of the pants and then even tens of thousands and this poor excuse for a human being turned them down. How can our system even allow such a ridiculous case to go to trial?

Another man actually brought a lawsuit against someone who saved him from choking. Apparently while in the process of aiding the man the Good Samaritan broke some of the man's ribs. Rather than thank his benefactor he turned around and sued him. I do believe in this situation the judge threw the case out, but it just goes to show you how far people will go in using our court system to gain a few bucks. When even the good will of individuals can be used against them in the legal system, we have got to admit that we are facing a severe problem.

We cannot permit a society in which every unforeseen event can be the cause for a lawsuit. Litigation has a time and place, but it has been allowed to run amok in our country. Common sense must be returned to the courts or we may have to enact legislation that will hold a plaintiff liable for the defendants' legal fees if they lose. If these practices are not halted now the result will be a nation where every inch is covered by warning signs and every person will have a coterie of lawyers following behind their every step.

One of the main things we need to do is to change the system. Tort reform is of the utmost essence. It is time to not only limit the actions of plaintiffs, but to go after lawyers who are abusing the courts. We need to establish parameters that better define what can constitute as liability. We can no longer allow the imaginations of the greedy to find ways in which they can turn innocent occurrences into cash rewards. Our nation suffers far too much from the costs of such unnecessary lawsuits. We as a nation must alter this atmosphere of litigiousness if we are ever to stop being fettered by its shackles.

POLITICS

In general the politics of the United States is intellectually bankrupt and morally corrupt, but what else do you expect it's a democracy? Yet, I look at this country from the local level to the national stage and I believe we can do better. As I write this we are in the midst of a presidential election. This leads me to ask, how many of you believe that the dozen or so serious candidates we had are actually the best that this country has to offer? All of those running are typical politicians. Most of those running have no moral certitude and are willing to switch positions depending on who the electorate is. Rather than give a litany of the lies, waffles, changed positions, and inconsistencies, let's just say that the politicians in this nation offer us little. Yet, I have to blame the public at large for this, because they do nothing to change this situation.

The people say they want change, but then want candidates with political experience. Virtually every person in this country that holds office has used politics as usual to gain that office. How do voters expect to get change when we elect those that are already part of the system? Honesty is met by cynicism, consistency isn't believed, and worst of all, we have come to accept politicians lying. We will never get change unless the people and the media stop allowing politics as usual. Until we do this we will not get real true leaders, but ineffective parrots who repeat what they think we want to hear.

I live in one of the most corrupt and heavily taxed states in the union. The state of New Jersey is practically ruled by the Democratic Party. Yet, time and time again the citizens of this state vote for the same people from the same politically corrupt machines. Somehow the voters in this state felt that electing Jon Corzine would change something. He is a tax and spend liberal who presupposes he knows better than the people of this state. We voted against an embryonic stem cell research center, one that he did the groundbreaking ceremony on before the election. But now that it has been voted down he is actually trying to fund the project by alternative means. He and our legislature also went against the majority of people in the state who wanted to maintain our death penalty, and, surprise, surprise, he raised taxes. The people of this state get what they deserve. We must stop looking to the politicians to change the way we are governed and find new places to get our leaders.

Essentially, the same elite attitude pervades our government on a national scale. To some degree every state also has much of the same problems. When our government tried to ram an amnesty bill on illegal immigration down our throats, it was only the blaring outcry of the American people that stopped its passage. The politicians thought in their infinite wisdom that they knew what was best for us. They also display this cavalier attitude in general. Nothing is done to change the problems facing Social Security, Medicare, and Medicaid. We need leaders, on both the right and the left, who are willing to speak their minds and hold fast to what they say. The continuous lies and politicizing of every single issue have turned most people off to politics. Democracies don't function well when citizens see little point in voting.

It is hard to have a serious debate when the varying sides can't even agree on the facts that they are debating. Liberals and conservatives are both guilty of this. Each side does its best to twist and tweak the facts and numbers that support their respective points of view. This makes it very hard for people to make decisions on issues. In order to understand any issue one has to navigate a maze of half-truths and misrepresentations to figure out what they think is best. Most citizens are too busy to spend this much time on politics and have little idea what it is they are voting for. Debates on TV are little more than a series of soundbites and gotcha questions. How does any of this make for an informed electorate? And that is just what we need to turn this country's politics around: an informed electorate.

Another major problem is negative campaign ads. Every election season the radio and television are littered with these annoying ads. The narrator's voice breaks into that accusatory tone and blasts away at the candidate under attack with a litany of their horrid offenses, and then at the end it says paid for by so and so, who isn't evil. When a candidate can't run on his or her own record that person is part of the problem. I'm not saying one can never point out the faults of an opponent, but we need people to run on what they will try to accomplish and their strengths as a person. Negative campaign ads are a significant cause of the apathy that voters have for our system in general. Why vote if all the candidates suck?

With the population turned off to politics in general it is hard to get the people involved. With the system so corrupt it is hard to get people with integrity to run for elected office. Candidates have to worry about every single misstep of their life being made public and exposed in the worst light possible. Look at how much time politicians spend refuting past mistakes and erroneous claims about their lives. Few people have the stomach to endure this vicious investigation into every minute detail of their lives. The system can not improve if only persons of suspect characters are willing to run. We also will never see candidates worthy of office if every untoward act of someone's life is exacerbated to make them appear as Hitler. None of us is perfect and we need to give politicians some leeway for being imperfect.

I would like to see less adversarial debate come back into American politics. It is so tiring to watch partisans of both sides accuse the other of worse wrong doing rather than debate the issue at hand. True discussion of issues has all but disappeared from the political life of

America. Instead we see short-spirited arguments that have little to do with what is actually being debated. We need solutions to the problems that we face and the current state of politics does little to find these solutions. Attacking those who are on the other side of an issue does not make sound policy; all it does is allow the system to continue as it has been.

Another of the major problems that corrupts our system is money. Money corrupts American politics in a number of ways. The most important is probably campaign financing. The millions it takes to run for office on a statewide or national scale is a retardant to the participation of many citizens. This high cost of running a campaign also puts our politicians in a position that is beholden to those who finance elections. On top of this it also allows those with great personal fortunes to run for office at whim, New York City Mayor Bloomberg and the aforementioned New Jersey Governor Corzine being two of the more prominent examples. The McCain- Feingold act has done little to alleviate these concerns. In fact, its unconstitutional restrictions on free speech have made things worse.

Already in this campaign for president we have seen the role of questionable money: Dishwashers who barely make the minimum wage donating thousands of dollars, criminals raising funds for a campaign, money bundled and donated in the names of others, and the bank rolls of lobbying groups that represent foreign nations and interests. How can all of this not prove that our system is broken? We need to alter the way in which we allow campaigns to be financed. We might also want to shorten them to reduce the cost of interminable election cycles. Possibly a method needs to be created that allows for public funding or the free use of the media during this process.

Clearly the corruption of bribery and kickbacks is also a significant problem that money causes in our system. In New Jersey the FBI went after a number of state and local officials in a bribery probe. Not one, not one, of the officials involved turned them down. If that doesn't show the pervasive corruption in our politics I don't know what would. Both liberals and conservatives are guilty in this matter. Yet, either side always tries to show that the other is more criminal than they are, rather than try to address the lack of morality that so many politicians have. Criminal penalties for the misuse of public funds should be far harsher than they are now. Abuse of the public trust is one of the most serious crimes possible, because it tears at the foundation upon which our society is supposed to be built.

Earmarks and the government's bloated budgets in general cause money to have an undue amount of influence on politics. We are no longer talking millions, but billions and even trillions of dollars in the coffers that our politicians dispense. Conflicts of interest are frequent with our elected officials. They have undue control of who gets what government funding. Too often we see this lead to nepotism and the needless waste of public dollars. How much of every dollar spent by government is wasted in unnecessary projects and programs that are designed to reward political cronies and associates? I feel the best way to deal with this problem is to look into a possible constitutional amendment allowing for a line item veto for the president. Many states already have such laws on the books; those that don't should get one.

Despite the faults I am pointing to in our system I actually do not think the current state of politics is any different than it has been for much of our nation's history. This is not saying much about those who have ruled us. Our country has become great not because of politicians, but in spite of them. There are few in the annals of American history that we can hold up as role models in the political field. If we are to navigate the future world we will need to have true leaders. We can not continue to have bitter partisanship dividing us. Unfortunately I see little room for the left and right to compromise on most issues we currently face. We also can not allow money to have such an undue influence on policy. It is time to start looking at the qualities that actually make for effective leadership. Usually those who want power are the last people in the world that we would want to place into positions of power. The current state of affairs in the U.S. certainly does not make it easy for our country to address the critical issues that face us in the coming years.

THE MILITARY

The United States of America has the best, most powerful, and most technologically advanced military that the world may ever have seen. It is imperative that we do everything in our power to ensure that our military stays in this position. We are posed with a world that is on the brink of collapse. Nations that do not appear as an overt threat today can morph in a very short amount of time into a grave danger to our country. We would be wise to keep our eyes open and our ability to defend ourselves strong. Since WWII America has had the power to use military force to build an empire, but rather than that we have chosen to use force only as a necessity. Clearly, some of our actions in that time can be questioned, but the minimally disproportionate use of our power, even in war, shows that America has been a good national citizen on the world stage. Few peoples in the history of the world with such extraordinary power relative to the other nations of the world would have acted in the way we have under these circumstances.

Most generals in history have been fighting the last war. It takes true vision to look ahead and deduce what the conflicts of the future may hold in store. The U.S. has to prepare for more than one type of battle in the future. We are now seeing in Iraq and Afghanistan the asymmetrical warfare we will see from certain types of enemies in the future. We must not forget, though, that there are other forms of fighting that will be necessary in the times to come. I'd prefer not to name any particular opponents, but anybody with knowledge of world affairs can assess which nations have the potential to confront the U.S. in a total war. Total war is a phrase that refers to the use of a complete society in the course of a conflict. WWI and WWII are probably the two best examples of such warfare. With the proliferation of weapons of mass destruction and of nuclear arms the concept of total war becomes truly frightening.

I hate war, but it would be foolish for any nation to not consider the possibility that fighting may be necessary from time to time. What would the world look like if we had chosen to remain neutral during WWII? How many more years would it have taken for slavery to be outlawed in the United States if we did not fight the Civil War? Combat should always be a last resort, but it must always remain an option. If we refuse to accept this then we will be at the mercy of any nation or group that threatens us. The U.S needs to remain in as advanced a position as we possibly can.

One of the biggest problems facing our military today is the lack of manpower. I feel that this is largely due to the constant portrayal of the current conflicts in the worst possible light. I can't tell you how many of my students have been under the notion that the current war is one of the most deadly in American history. This idea permeates our culture as a whole. Only those who are educated beyond the mainstream media have any concept of how ludicrous this idea is. Every soldier lost or injured is a tragedy, but in historical terms Iraq is a war that is very low in casualties. If the nightly news had portrayed our losses in WWI in such a way as they portray our losses in Iraq the country might never have fought in another war again. In about six months of actual combat in 1918 we lost around 50,000 dead. Could you imagine what CNN and *The New York Times* would do with figures like that?

With this fear of service permeating so many people in our society it is a wonder that anyone signs up for military duty at all. Yet, day in and day out we see numerous fine young men and women enter the military. As a teacher I have had personal experience with this. When my students have told me that they are considering the military I have always told them two things. One is that they need to think about the possibility of being killed or injured. The other is that our country needs people in the armed forces and if that is what they think they should do, then go for it. America has the weapons to fight, but they are meaningless if we do not have the boots on the ground to control a given area.

On the topic of manpower I feel it important to consider one of the more controversial issues pertaining to those who serve in the military. Specifically I am referring to the issue of gays in the military. I have always thought that this prohibition is unnecessary. Self-respecting adults would not jeopardize their career for some sexual encounter, and when they do there are already laws and regulations to handle this. Any person who can meet the physical and character standards posed by our armed forces should have the opportunity to serve our nation. When I hear stories of completely capable interpreters of Arabic being tossed out of the service when they are in dire need, I question the efficacy of prohibiting openly gay people from serving. We need every person that we can get, and if that is true now wait until some truly terrible conflicts arise.

Part of what makes our military so formidable is our extremely advanced technology. Few nations even possess a fraction of the capabilities that we have. Yet, it is key to our ability to defend ourselves to maintain this technological advantage we have at this time. Therefore, I think it is imperative that we continue to develop and master new weapon systems. In order to keep costs reasonable we must utilize the great minds that we have available to create programs that are pertinent to the challenges the world may pose and viable in terms of their practicality. Technology is the best way for us to reduce the amount of troops necessary for a conflict and the amount of peril that they will encounter on the battlefield.

In the current geopolitical climate I feel one of the technologies that the U.S. must employ is a missile defense system. We are currently in the early stages of such a program. The technology and science necessary for such a program are within our grasp. Therefore it is imperative that we do all that we reasonably can to make such a defense a reality. It is only a matter of time until the likes of Iran and North Korea have the ability to strike our nation at will. We no longer live in an age where two oceans complicate the potential for an attack. As time goes on more and more countries will become advanced in the deployment of sophisticated technological weaponry. We would be foolish to trust our safety entirely to the goodwill of other countries.

When most think of technology they often forget the power of tactical innovation. This is not only manifested in maneuvers in combat, but in the ways our troops are trained to deal with the population in a given theatre of conflict. Many of my former students who have returned from active duty have told me that they have not been taught even the rudiments of the language of the local people in the area that they were fighting. This not only makes their interaction with the population physically dangerous, but it increases the difficulties of communicating a message that will win hearts and minds. This is especially true of conflicts where our enemies are using asymmetrical warfare. Policies need to be implemented that familiarize our troops with the cultural, religious, and social practices of the residents of any area of conflict. The wars of the twenty-first century will be fought as much on the battlefield as they will be fought in the media.

One of the salient problems with our national defense that has been exposed in the Iraq and Afghan wars has been our lack of reliable intelligence. Future conflicts will rely more heavily on intelligence than any wars that we have fought in the past. This is especially true when considering the potential for nations or groups to acquire the use of weapons of mass destruction. It is impossible to assess the threats posed to us when we do not have actionable information provided by operatives working within the societies that hope to attack us. Our intelligence agencies were stripped to the bone from the 1970s to September 11th,

2001. We have to make up for that loss of time with intensive efforts to establish intelligence forces which can operate in covert manners that permit for our understanding of the nature and types of threats our enemies pose.

The way our troops are treated by the Armed Forces is also one of the most important issues surrounding our military. I was incensed when one of my former students told me that he had to prove that he was injured in combat. For his protection I must remain vague. There was no question as to how he had received his injuries. Yet, in order to get medical and rehabilitative treatment he had to show that he had been injured. I do not know what the purpose of such a requirement was, but I felt that this was an insult to him as a veteran. His wounds were not exceptionally severe, but he still needed to have the military aid in his recovery. I don't care if our troops get a paper cut filing documents in the States; any care that they need must be administered with the greatest efficiency and least hassle as possible to them. They are the ones sacrificing for us to maintain our freedom. The scandalous conditions at some of our military medical facilities exemplify the fact that we are failing those who have put their lives on the line for the greater good.

All institutions have their problems, but I feel that our military overall is an exemplary force. We must maintain a constant vigilance to ensure that it stays this way. While we do that we must continue to provide the best care and training to our fighting men and women. We also must give them the best possible equipment and technology that we can. To do anything less is to short change them and the nation as a whole. I remember Eisenhower's admonition to avoid the military industrial complex, and I think we must watch that we never slide into such a despotism. Yet, we can never lose sight of the fact that well-trained armed forces with the greatest level of sophisticated technological equipment provide the best possible national defense.

ENGLISH IS THE LANGUAGE OF THE UNITED STATES OF AMERICA

This is another one of those issues where the liberals like to call their opponents names. In this case it is usually epithets like racist or xenophobe. Somehow, many on the left seem to think that it is prejudiced to state the truth, that English is the cultural and de facto language of this nation. They also miss the point that it is very hard to succeed in this country without a working command of the English language. I am not suggesting that we necessarily make English the official language, but that we simply stop catering to those who speak foreign languages. It doesn't take a genius to figure out that it is harder to learn a new language when one never has to use it. So, it is those who wish to facilitate the learning of English who actually want to aid newly arrived immigrants.

First of all, it must be understood that it is very hard to learn a new language after the age of twenty-five for most people. I am not suggesting that we remove the use of foreign languages from our society. Quite the contrary, I would find that odious and oppressive. What I do want to do, though, is stop unnecessarily aiding the use of foreign tongues. Many of the liberal programs and ideas about helping foreigners actually retard these people's ability to learn English. The main place that we see this is in the school systems.

I have had personal experience with English as a second language programs. As an educator I can tell you they are the worst things for these young students. In many cases these students spend years in these classrooms and learn little English. Young people, especially elementary students, learn languages best from osmosis. They do not learn it by studying the language, but by living it. When they are stuck in a classroom where they are not experiencing English they are losing valuable time in the learning process. If these programs are to exist at all the students should be limited to no more than one year in the program, unless they have special education needs.

Students learn best when immersed in a language. If you have ever traveled abroad you should recognize this. I learned more Spanish in Chile and Argentina in two weeks than I did in two years of Spanish classes in high school. I had a similar experience in Germany, Switzerland, and Austria with the German language, but that also had a twist to the story. I had studied German a bit on my own since about the sixth grade. I also would speak a little with my Poppa. I also believe I took my first German class in college prior to this trip. Yet, while talking with people in German in Europe I would use words I knew I had never studied. I also would understand some words that I didn't have in my vocabulary. At the time it made no sense to me, yet when I took my second German class in college the mystery was solved. As I was reading a passage out loud my professor asked me where I had studied German before. I told her in college. She then asked if I had ever learned German anywhere else. I said that I had learned a bit from my Poppa and probably his dad too, my Great Grandpa. I then asked her why she wanted to know this. She told me that I was speaking with a Low German accent and that they taught High German in school. I then told her that my Great Grandpa's family was from southern Germany. What is stranger still is this brought back memories of my childhood. Prior to my Great Grandpa dying, when I was five years old, we used to spend a lot of time together. One of the things we used to do was go for walks and visit his friends on the block. What I now realized, and vaguely remember, is that he and some of his friends not only spoke German to each other but thought it was cute to teach me to speak in German. It now became clear to me why I had resisted saying certain German sounds that my first professor had tried to teach the class: I preferred to speak in Low German rather than in the High German that I was being taught.

Now there are two points to these stories, beyond me taking a walk down memory lane. The first point is that language is learned best when one is surrounded by it. The second is that language is absorbed by a very young mind. I had not spoken much German in almost twenty years, yet my mind had retained it in its rudimentary form. Too bad I never learned enough to speak either Spanish or German fluently, but I can at least get by. Whenever I go to a foreign country I always make it my business to learn how to say hello/goodbye, please, thank you, excuse me, and a few numbers if I can. I have to admit it has helped my relations with the locals in every country I've been to except France.

Hopefully, these points and stories clarify why it is so essential to learn English to the best of one's ability if they are going to reside in the United States. This applies equally to those who are born into families that speak English in the home. How one speaks and their vocabulary reveals their intellectual and cultural understanding. Opportunities are lost to those who do not excel as much as they can in learning English. If I were to move abroad I would have no expectation that that country would cater to me by translating everything into English.

As a historian I have no fear that any other language will replace English in this country. Even if the first generation is unable, or unwilling, to learn our language the second generation always does. Yet, I do think that we have gone too far in trying to accommodate people who do not speak English. Why don't we try harder to teach new immigrants the language? We do them no service by providing everything from education to government documents in their own tongue. The best way to help people who come to this country is to teach them our language. It is the common thread of our culture, society, and our democracy.

HEALTHCARE

As far as I am concerned this is one of the most dangerous domestic issues of our time. This is especially true in this election year. Few topics illuminate the differences between liberals and conservatives as this. Candidate after candidate on the Democratic side talks about universal healthcare. This socialist idea has the power to bankrupt this nation. Government-run healthcare would be as much or more of a failure than the government-run schools, post office, Social Security, and welfare programs. Clearly something does have to be done to reduce the costs of healthcare. It is also important for this country to find a way to get those without health insurance a method to be covered. But we must resist any efforts to turn the system of healthcare over to the government.

Outside of the military, the interstate highway system, NASA, and NOAA, what has the government ever done right? If you want to ensure higher healthcare costs and a reduction in quality, hand the system over to the federal government. Those who support socialized medicine are either ignorant or have a vested interest in the plan. What will bureaucrats do to improve healthcare in the United States? Once they have their greedy, incompetent hands in healthcare we will never be able to get it back!

America has the best doctors and care available. The only fault in our system is the high cost. Yes, that is a significant problem, but getting the government involved will only ruin healthcare. Look at the socialized systems of Europe and Canada. They have long waiting lists, a lack of doctors and healthcare professionals, and the costs are bankrupting their nations. When they need complicated procedures many people in those countries come to the United States. We have a great system; the problem is for those that are unable to afford care. So, let us find a way to include them without destroying the best healthcare system in the world.

Some of the high costs incurred by Americans are due to the socialist systems abroad. Their reduced costs for medication and equipment cause companies to charge higher prices here. This is especially true of medication. Another major cause of exorbitant prices is liability. The great expense of lawsuits and malpractice insurance drives up the cost of healthcare in the U.S. Sen. John Edwards, who ran on his platform of "two Americas," is a millionaire for this exact reason. He is one of those lawyers who has made a fortune from lawsuits. Medical practitioners are having to pass along the costs that they face in malpractice insurance onto their patients. This puts a premium on cost before the patients ever arrive to receive care.

Americans are over-medicated. We take medicine and antibiotics without real cause. I can demonstrate this with an event from my own life. I know that many from other states do not realize just how much woodlands New Jersey has, despite the state being the most densely populated state in the union. Several years ago I was doing my daily check for ticks and lo and behold I found one on my leg. It was just starting to penetrate my skin. So, I plucked it off with some tweezers and put it in a little bottle. I went to a medi-center and tried to have the tick submitted for testing for Lyme disease, which is very prevalent in New Jersey. The staff refused to take the tick for testing unless I had an examination by the doctor. I didn't see why that was necessary, but my need to have the test done caused me to relent. The doctor looked at the spot on my leg and could barely discern it from several other spots I had in the same area. Needless to say, she proposed that I take antibiotics. Knowing a bit about Lyme disease I knew that a ring would appear around the bite if I had contracted the contagion. So, I refused and said I would wait until the ring appeared or the test came back positive. After about two weeks I received the results and the tick was negative. Yet, the doctor still suggested that I take the antibiotics anyway. Obviously, I refused. This is an example of why the unnecessary use of antibiotics is causing strains of super bacteria to form. Medications should only be used as a last resort or when prudence suggests.

As a teacher I see the over-prescription of medication and antibiotics all the time. Obviously, not being a medical professional I keep my opinions on these matters to myself when in school. Yet, I have seen students started on ADHD medications as early as four years old. From what I know of children as an uncle and an educator, I find it hard to grasp how this need for medication can be ascertained at such a young age. Trust me, I have seen students that need the prescriptions that they are getting, but oftentimes the problems are from a lack of discipline at home. The costs to this nation from these types of treatments are exorbitant.

When doctors prescribe medicines the second people get a cough or a sniffle, they diminish the effectiveness of their patient's immune system. We also have to consider the influence of incentives offered to physicians by the pharmaceutical companies for the use of their products. I find it hard to believe that these incentives do not corrupt the integrity of professional decisions. Why is it that I have noticed that the people who are the healthiest spend the least time at the doctor's office? I don't think that applies to children, but to adults. I fear doctors and will only go when I can no longer function. In twenty years I have been prescribed medication only twice. Any attempt to address the high costs of our healthcare system needs to concentrate on the reduction of redundant and unnecessary care. Medical professionals need to make our healthcare decisions along with their patients, but believing that all of the economic incentive to provide care has not led to the excessive use of the system is naïve.

Drug-resistant bacteria are becoming an increasing problem for healthcare facilities around the world. The recent outbreak of MRSA is just one of a plethora of examples. Diseases get stronger as we over-prescribe medication. Experts in the field of medicine must create an outline of the means by which we can reduce our dependence on manufactured medications. Addressing the causes of illness is as important as addressing its symptoms. We must also look to the inclusion of non-traditional treatments (by Western standards) in our healthcare system. Many other cultures have a lot to teach us about how we approach sickness.

I fear that the socialization of medical practice in this country will reduce the options available for Americans in dealing with their healthcare. In our current capitalist system we have innumerable choices for treatment. If we allow incompetent bureaucrats to manage healthcare they will decide what is and is not an acceptable means for treating disease. What do you think will guide their decision-making process more, cost or the general welfare of the patients? Who also will be first at the chopping block of budget considerations? Personally I believe it will be the elderly and those who need chronic care. Again, look to some of the suggestions being posited in the European debates on cutting healthcare costs. Some have even gone as far as suggesting euthanasia for those who are not terminally ill, but who have a poor quality of life. I would like to see who determines what the quality of life for someone else is and how they come about making their decisions. None of these draconian measures has been put into place as of now, but how long until they start to come to fruition?

Alternative medicine is almost certain to get short-changed in any government-run program. Bureaucrats usually only deal with what they can understand. Bureaucrats also do not like to deal with the intangible. If you think it is hard to get insurance companies to pay for alternative and innovative care now, just wait until the incompetent government takes over. Many innovative techniques prove to vary in effect from person to person and therefore make quantitative evidence of their efficacy difficult to ascertain. Socialized medicine will leave us at the mercy of people who are not healthcare professionals to make decisions on what is, and is not, appropriate care. I'd rather maintain my freedom to choose what care I get and what I will pay for.

The effect of liability on our system will only be exacerbated by the nationalization of our system. Imagine how government paper-pushers will deal with perceived liability. The ability to sue will either be written out of legality if we nationalize healthcare or it will become a retardant to innovation and study. The bureaucrats will stifle any attempt at new treatments that do not completely insulate them from recourse by patients. I have seen a documentary on the Ebola virus a number of times. In the documentary several African doctors come up with an unorthodox method for treating the disease. All of the African doctors think it has the potential to work. Yet, they do not even approach the American and European doctors with the plan. Why? Because the Westerners would perceive the plan as unethical. Eventually, the African doctors carry out their idea. They suppose it would be a good idea to draw blood from the small group of people who had contracted Ebola, but had survived the disease. They then transfused the blood into those patients who were ill with the deadly virus. The plan worked, with quite a few lives being saved. Despite the success of the experiment the African doctors were chastised by their Western counterparts for their abrogation of protocol. Protocol, not the lives of those who were ill, was foremost in the minds of the Westerners. How much more so would this propriety be extended if we put cold-hearted bureaucrats in the positions to decide how we are treated?

The most difficult part of dealing with this issue is trying to deduce how we will afford to extend healthcare to all without losing the quality of the treatment we receive. Reducing costs and unnecessary care can certainly make this prospect more of a reality, but we have to wonder if this will be enough. If it is not we are faced with a dilemma. Do we continue with the system as it is or do we find some new means to fund the uninsured? Many methods for including those without insurance have been tried in several different states. These plans and those ideas still untried need to be researched. I wish I could say that I had the answer to these questions, but as of now I do not. What I can say adamantly is that we should never socialize medicine in this country. If you think the system is broken now you will wish we had it back when it is compared to what the government would do with healthcare.

GLOBAL CLIMATE CHANGE

Global climate change has become an extremely controversial issue. Frankly, I don't think it should be controversial. Sadly, the scientific debate on this issue has been hijacked by politicians and partisans on both sides. We also have seen the profit motive enter into the picture. I have examined the subject of climate change in depth. The most difficult part of the problem is assessing the vast array of things that contribute to what creates the Earth's climate. It is also very hard to ascertain how to investigate the past conditions we have had on our planet. The interplay of these generators of our climate poses a significant challenge to anyone looking into this critical issue as well.

Climate change does seem to be occurring. The questions are, though, how much are human beings contributing to it and how much of it is natural? This is where the debate has become controversial. Many on the left have gone as far as calling those who question the human ingredient in climate change the equivalent of Holocaust deniers or those who maintain the Earth is flat. Many prominent scientists do not readily accept that people are the main cause of this phenomenon and they point to natural mechanisms that may generate the same results. Still others seem to believe that a combination of manmade and natural causes may be at the root of our changing climate. If I had to put forth my opinion at this moment I would place myself with the latter group, yet I do not think it is possible at this point to quantify what is caused by human activity and what is due to nature.

Often I hear those who are opponents and proponents of the idea of global climate change site specific weather events as evidence for their point of view. Opponents usually site a record cold snap or freak snowstorm as evidence against this theory, and proponents of the idea point towards events like Hurricane Katrina to support their claims. Yet, it is both who are failing to understand the process of science. We need to establish a factual basis for our claims, not establish an amalgamation of evidence to create a Tower of Babel theory. Figuring out how to establish these facts is one of the major problems we encounter when studying this issue. Even scientifically acceptable procedures can be subject to a great variety of interpretations. Data of ice cores, tree rings, sunspots, and human records cannot be used in isolation. Every piece of the puzzle seems to add to the complexity of determining what is a normal part of our planet's climate cycles and what is an aberration.

What has annoyed me in my attempts to research this subject is the apparent partisanship that affects almost every study I have examined. The facts themselves are questioned in almost every case, essentially reducing the findings to opinions. Advocates of global warming site the dramatic uptick in CO_2 since the beginning of the Industrial Revolution to support their claims, and dissenters attack the validity of the findings that there has even been such a dramatic increase in CO_2. Opponents to man-induced climate change point to the variability of the Earth's climate in the past and proponents of the theory try to show how this current change is accelerated by the added emissions from human activity. All I seek is the truth, but I feel that I am in a maze of facts, anecdotes, and partisan half-truths.

Many liberals have resorted to propaganda to get their point across. Movies like *The Day After Tomorrow* and *An Inconvenient Truth* are probably the two most prominent examples. The former is nothing more than a ridiculous story in the vein of Hollywood. The latter, for all its imperfections, is at least a more realistic portrayal of what climate change may mean for mankind. Yet, I have to severely criticize Al Gore's gross exaggerations and his unscientific conclusions. We do not need more hyperbole in this debate but sober facts. Climate change appears to be a reality and the human race needs to react to it whether it is induced by man, nature, or both.

So, let us look to the facts as they stand by themselves. Let us examine the issue away from the politics and partisanship. What is it that is occurring? When we look to the ages we see that Earth has not always had the same climate. In fact, we see that it has undergone extreme variations in the past and that some of these great changes have occurred in historical times. To be honest it is difficult to even understand if the climate that we consider normal is what Earth usually experiences, or if what we know as our climate is the abnormality. The period we live in is in the immediate aftermath of what we call the little ice age. This was a period from around 1450 to 1850; prior to that we call the climate the medieval warm period. Such extreme variations in a one thousand-year period tend to lead one to question the climactic stability that so many assume is Earth's norm.

Mankind has only existed for a minute period of the Earth's existence. Our historical records are even shorter. The time in which we have scientifically observed our planet's behavior is even shorter still. So, how is it that we will determine if we are a major contributor to the climate change that seems to be happening right now? I think that this is where the controversy begins. Liberals want to react to their gut instinct that six-and-a-half billion of us may be causing the problem, and conservatives want to find out whether we are a major cause of this change before we alter the day-to-day existence of society based on inconclusive science. I feel that neither is the correct approach. We cannot wait until the science is conclusive; it probably will never be. We also cannot turn society on its head and haphazardly stab into the dark, attempting to trumpet every new practice that we hope will "save the Earth." New types of light bulbs and different behaviors might reduce our impact on our environment, but they will not radically reduce how we affect the world. If we are causing this problem it has been a long time in coming. Any means to diminish our effects on how we change the climate can be gradually worked into the life of everyday society, even if we have to add a little kick to what we do

I feel it is important to have at least a rudimentary exposition of the facts and theories involved in global climate change. First and foremost has to be the consideration of the sun. It doesn't take a genius to deduce that that big yellow star in the sky might be a key generator in any climate change. It is also important to note that it does appear that the cycles of the sun's magnetic field cause sunspots. Some studies show a strong correlation between Earth's climate and these sunspots. Sunspots cycle every eleven years; they also can vary in intensity over the course of centuries. Some of the most intense sunspots occurred in the late 1990s and early 2000s. Many of the hottest years on record are to be found in this timeframe. Conversely, the nadir of the little ice age appears to have come when sunspots were almost non-existent. This is not a scientific law, but it does need to be understood more completely in order for us to understand climate change.

Volcanic eruptions also can cause great variations in Earth's atmosphere. This can happen in at least two ways: either a single giant eruption or more numerous minor eruptions. The super volcanoes can affect Earth over a number of years. Increased volcanic activity as a whole can cause long-term climactic change. Twice in modern history super volcanoes have caused dramatic effects on the weather around the world. The first time it was the 1815 eruption of Tambora, in Indonesia, which led to the year without a summer in 1816 across most of the northern hemisphere. This caused major crop failures and less ominous events like different colored snows. The super-eruption of Krakatoa in 1883, also in Indonesia, disrupted the climate in a less dramatic manner than the Tambora eruption. Around 70,000 years ago the blast from Toba, yet again in Indonesia, led to such dramatic climate change that the primitive race of humans may have had its population reduced to about 5,000 individuals worldwide.

What is very significant when looking at volcanoes is their byproduct of sulfur dioxide. SO2, due to its molecular composition, acts almost like a mirror, reflecting light back into space before it has had a chance to warm the surface of the earth. It appears that this effect is so powerful that it has even been able to negate the power of high-intensity sunspots. This effect only lasts for several years, so only a long-term increase in overall volcanic activity can be attributable to climate change, and that really only when one is dealing with cooling. Obviously. the general trend we are seeing right now seems to be one tending towards warming. Maybe we'll get lucky and some extra volcanic activity will spew out some fresh sulfur dioxide into the atmosphere and all our problems will go away, except for those who happen to live near or around these volcanoes.

When trying to establish the past climactic record of the Earth several different sources are used to study the planet's history. Chief among these are tree rings, ice cores, ocean sediment, and historical records. All of these studies have their place, yet each of them has its problems. Historical records are incomplete and only show a snapshot of one specific area in a specific time frame. Ice cores and ocean sediments are fairly stable, but the enormous complexity of deducing evidence from them is still a challenge to scientists and a cause for debate. Tree rings, or dendrochronology, is fraught with problems. First it has to be established from what period of time the tree existed, and then the actual study of the rings can be questioned. As I have mentioned before I have worked with trees for nearly twenty years. I find many of the suppositions of dendrochronologists to be faulty at best. Their assumption that wider rings account for more moisture and thinner rings less moisture is too simplistic. I have seen years in which excessive rainfall has caused significantly less growth in trees, not more. All things considered, I find these studies to have validity, but they are all open to a wide variety of interpretation.

Another factor in this debate is the role of methane in the climate of the earth. Vast pockets of methane exist under the ocean's floors. Some of these pockets release slowly, others can burst forth very suddenly. Methane has twenty-six times the power to act as a greenhouse-trapping gas as does carbon dioxide. Quite comically, cow flatulence may be one of the most prominent sources of methane now being produced in our world. Many models that are supposed to predict the future changes in Earth's climate do not include either methane or sulfur dioxide in their data. This essentially reduces the reliability of such models to forecast the changes that we may experience in coming years.

Ultimately what does all this mean in terms of how mankind addresses the issue of global climate change? I would tend to say it puts us between the do-nothing crowd and the environmentalist whackos telling me to use only one sheet of toilet paper when I go to the bathroom. I don't know what their bodies are expelling, but one sheet just isn't going to suffice for me. Yet, it would probably be best overall, even if climate change has no human contribution, to begin to alter our more wasteful habits. Making changes to our daily routines that conserve energy and resources is not only practical, but, I believe, moral. God did not put us here to consume the Earth and its produce like ravenous parasites that take and take until the host is denuded of all vestiges of life. I feel the use of our energy is such an important issue with separate political issues to be considered that I have devoted a chapter to it later in this book.

GAY RIGHTS

This topic is another one about which the liberals like to call anyone who opposes their position names. In this case the name is homophobe. The implication is that one fears homosexuals and homosexuality. I am sure that this is true of some, but it is possible to hold the thought that homosexuality is not morally right without being afraid of gays. It is also possible to believe that it is immoral, but not illegal. Many of the issues that surround the place of gays in society as a whole make it very tough to strike a balance between what is legally fair to gays and when state acceptance of homosexuality becomes a religious imposition to others. This is particularly true of same sex marriages and civil unions. It is also important when considering the right to association that private groups, organizations, and individuals have.

My position on the issue of gay marriage is simple: It is not mentioned in the Constitution, therefore it is a right left unto the states. That is why we need a constitutional amendment that establishes marriage as a union of one man and one woman. Without such an amendment activists will use the courts to force their idea of marriage onto the rest of society. Many supporters of gay marriage say that an amendment establishing heterosexual marriage is doing the same thing. I beg to differ. Until recently marriage in our culture has only been viewed as a heterosexual bond. Look to polygamy and this becomes clear. It is the gay marriage supporters who are trying to redefine what has been the tradition in our society. This is why nothing defining marriage was put into our Constitution; they never thought it needed to be defined.

If we legalize gay marriage we have to legalize polygamy and any other union people may try to create. Without a constitutional amendment this is exactly what will happen. Remember the sit-in that the children of polygamists had in Utah? If those who support gay marriage say that tradition should not stop them from forming unions, others will use the same argument to defend their unions. Legally, the way things stand now, they are right. Each state could determine what they accept as marriage. Yet, we can be sure activists will move from state to state challenging the laws. A couple will get married in Massachusetts and then move to Kansas to challenge the laws there, and so on and so forth. Eventually by judicial fiat it will become the law of the land.

So, is there a way to compromise? I know some will always view such a compromise as a violation of their rights, but I disagree. If you notice, I make no calls to what the majority thinks or about the lifestyles of gays. These are rather poor arguments and resort to generalities that have no place in law, and frankly are usually prejudiced towards gays. The best solution is some form of civil unions. I feel these unions don't have to be offered exclusively to gays, but can be extended to other people as well. What I envision will encompass many of the issues that adversely affect gays under the law, namely, inheritance, hospital visitation, insurance, and finances.

My main problem with gay marriage is that they call it marriage. This is the only religious institution that the government is involved in; for the state to redefine it is a violation of my first amendment rights. Finding an alternative legal way to ensure that gays are treated fairly is the option I think best. Therefore I think we should push for a constitutional amendment that defines marriage as between one man and one woman, but does not preclude civil unions. Obviously, such an institution would be used by gays, but they are not the only ones who could benefit. Relationships of a non-sexual nature could also be recognized. Each state would have to figure out its own specifics. The type of recognition I see is civil unions for gays and a civil registry for others. The main point of this idea is to have legal recognition of certain rights that are now exclusively in the realm of marriage. Two friends who bought a house can register and protect their rights; if they are personally close they can confer other rights to one another. Many of these laws probably exist, but this may eliminate some of the red tape and costs involved. This is an idea that is still in its infancy.

Another persistent problem for gays is adoption. When a homosexual naturally becomes a guardian, say in the case of the death of a sibling, I feel there is no legal reason to deny them of this position if they are fit to parent. Personally, I believe the optimal situation for children is a stable mother/father household, but that is not always possible. When the state looks to adoption this should be the first choice. Yet, when there are not enough people to meet this situation, stable, loving parents should be sought. If this means single parents or gay parents this is better than institutional upbringing. A loving family, no matter how non-traditional, is better than the cold hands of the state or a home. No matter how effective these institutions are they can't match a loving household.

One of the hardest rights to balance is the right of gays to work and associate. This is especially true of churches and organizations that do not view homosexuality as moral. Should the government be able to force groups to accept members that do not share their common beliefs? This question essentially comes down to the private nature of any group. Private organizations should be able to choose who their members and workers are. We see the common sense in preventing men from joining women's clubs. It is acceptable to require someone to be Chinese if they want to join a Chinese organization. So, forcing a church to hire gays if homosexuality is against its tenets should be equally unacceptable. Yet, when a group accepts public money or assistance they lose this right. Association with government support entails the all-encompassing equality that is at the basis of our Constitution. Obviously, there are some situations in which these rights will be less black and white and more nuanced, but I think the courts could handle it. (Well, maybe not the 9th Circuit!)

One of the more disturbing trends that surround gay rights has been moves to govern or restrict language. Canada and some Western European countries have in essence made it illegal for people to state that homosexuality is wrong. Laws of this nature are usually referred to as hate speech laws. I also deal with "hate speech" in my chapter on Civil Rights. These laws are fundamentally against the First Amendment. We have the right to free speech; laws that protect people from verbal abuse are sufficient to protect people. Claiming that the mere debate of a person's morality is hate speech is absurd. I know it is hard for many on the left to realize, but not everybody has the same beliefs as them, and not everybody who disagrees with their world view is an unenlightened cretin. Quite the contrary, most of us who view homosexuality as immoral try to discuss the issue with respect and compassion. The government should not be able to inhibit my right to express my beliefs if they do not threaten anyone. Claiming that the simple discussion of one's morality is an attack or affront is not only childish but nonsensical.

One of the issues that I feel necessary to include with this chapter is the rights of the so-called transsexual and transgender. Since I can barely even grasp the concept I find it hard to look at the issue. It is one thing to engage in a behavior that some consider immoral; it is quite another to surgically or medically change one's gender and ask me to accept it. Yes, they do have rights, but where do our rights to react or respond to such extreme behavior come into play? I have not ever consciously spoken to a person who has undergone such a procedure, but I don't know how I would feel or respond if I ever do.

I feel that the rights of gays have improved over the last several decades. How much more they need to be extended, if at all, is a question our society will be continually dealing with for some time. It is my hope for all people to live as freely as possible, but we have to avoid creating a foundationless society. We also have to ensure that we do not disrupt valuable traditions and institutions at the almighty altar of the individual. People do not have a right to never be uncomfortable. Freedom does not mean the right to do anything at any time. Part of a democracy is dealing with people who are different from one another. Attempting to balance the rights of individuals and the society as a whole is probably the most difficult and continuous process we have to engage in within this system.

THE PRESIDENTIAL ELECTION OF 2008

As I write this, the candidates for either major party are not set in stone. Yet, the Republican nominee has been all but decided and the Democrats have Hillary Clinton and Barack Obama fighting ferociously for their party's nod. John McCain seems to be the prospective Republican in the race and the two Democratic candidates are so similar that the choice of either of them is irrelevant. Being a conservative I am obviously not gleeful that John McCain will represent the Republicans barring some extraordinary turn of events, but it is beyond a shadow of a doubt that he would do better than either of the socialist train wrecks that will represent the Democrats. I especially believe this when it comes to the prosecution of the war. McCain may not be the best possible president, but Hillary or Obama would undoubtedly become the worst president since Jimmy Carter.

Aside from the many domestic issues that confront our nation we face a war that we cannot afford to lose. Mr. Obama has stated that he wants to end the war in Iraq as soon as possible. He has even used it to contrast himself with Senator McCain. Senator Obama even referred negatively to John McCain's willingness to stay the course in this conflict if it took a hundred years. This is the problem with the left: Despite the hyperbole, we need to fight this war for as long as it takes; time limits are not an option. They also fail to realize that this conflict is not isolated to Afghanistan and Iraq. It will morph from place to place and time to time. The Islamo-fascists are not going to disappear, regardless of what happens in Iraq. This is a cultural phenomenon that exists in dozens and dozens of countries and we must meet these threats wherever they present themselves. And Senator

Clinton has proven herself equally unable to confront these threats. She has held just about every position on the war possible, from voting to invade Iraq to pulling out of the country to partially pulling out of the nation to a number of other positions she has held due to polling and political expediency. Neither of the Democrats has a credible vision when it comes to what we will do in Iraq, Afghanistan, or the War on Terror as a whole. Obama is consistent, but consistently wrong, and Mrs. Clinton will say or do anything so long as the latest opinion poll says it is the most popular position held by the public on any given day.

Rather than rehash every issue I will only address those that serve to best show the differences that exist between those who may ascend to the presidency at this most critical time. Before I address the domestic issues I would like to take a brief overview of foreign policy beyond the War on Terror. The Democrats will project weakness onto the world stage. This is especially true of Obama. He has already said that he will sit down with the likes of Raul Castro and Ahmadinejad without any preconditions. Not only is this foolish, but it is naïve. Leaders of this sort cannot be trusted and any moves toward diplomacy must be initiated with their making concrete steps that permit for a real dialogue. Dictators do not have a great track record when it comes to honoring agreements. Iran has already backed out of a number of deals they have made with the Western powers. Meeting with the president of the United States of America will be used as a propaganda tool by these despotic regimes. In fact, the diplomatic victory it will hand them will be detrimental to our future negotiations on the concerns we have with these respective nations. Senator Clinton at least understands this basic point. Yet, she would put military action so far off the table that it will cease to be a credible course of action. I see little chance in Iran backing away from its development of nuclear weapons without this possibility. If the Western powers fail to stop Iran then Israel will have to take unilateral action. Only an idiot could fail to see how this would further destabilize the Middle East and probably lead to an all-out war.

Both Democratic candidates, and possibly Senator McCain, will make the mistake of signing a treaty similar to the Kyoto Treaty. If you think jobs are leaving the country now, wait until something like Kyoto goes into effect. We already have a great deal of trouble keeping the wages of our workers competitive with nations like China and India. The hindrance on our economy that will be the result of some global warming agreement would be insurmountable in the market place. This is especially true when one considers the fact that these types of agreement put almost all of the burdens on the major Western powers and Japan. Any treaty we sign needs to treat the economies of the world in the most equitable manner possible. Anything short of this will be economic suicide for the West.

A few of the domestic issues we face should suffice to show how disastrous the Democratic candidates would be. Both Obama and Clinton are intent on destroying the economy. Their answer to the bloated federal budget is to raise taxes rather than reduce spending. They speak of corporations as if they are the enemy of the people instead of their employers. The candidates for the Democrats want to raise corporate taxes despite the fact that we have one of the highest rates in the industrialized world. They talk of raising taxes on the rich, but the figure that determines if one is rich precipitously drops every time they speak. By the time they're done, rich will be defined as having some money under your mattress and some loose change in the seat of your couch. They want to double the capital gains tax. Not only has this money been taxed already, but what do they think that will do to the stock market? Typical of the left, they are anti-capitalist, anti-business, and favor tax and spend policies. Their recipe for the economy would return us to the days of the late 1970s.

The true test of the Democrats' socialism comes when we look at healthcare. They want to turn the system that provides the best treatments in the world over to the government. Hillary and Barack vie with one another to see just how much control the federal government will have in our healthcare decisions. Senator Clinton has even gone as far as suggesting that the government will garnish people's wages if they do not buy health insurance. Yes, I will admit that the greatest failing in how we operate our medical system is cost, but handing the system over to the government will ensure poorer quality care and a reduction of efficiency. It could even lead to higher costs. If your Lexus gets a flat tire, you don't trade it in for a bicycle.

One of the more important jobs the next president will have is the probable appointing of one to two justices to the Supreme Court. McCain may not make a perfect choice, but he is certain to do better than choosing someone like Ruth Bader Ginsburg. Either Democrat will choose a leftist activist justice that will look to foreign and international law to interpret the American Constitution. Either Democrat would appoint justices that will make law rather than enforce it. Senators Obama and Clinton, in short, would make selections to our Supreme Court that will negatively impact our nation for decades to come. Look at what the liberals have done with eminent domain. It is essential to the health of this republic that we get justices who know how to read our Constitution.

One of the biggest problems that conservatives have with McCain was his stance on illegal immigration in the past. Regardless if he will admit it or not, the bill he cosponsored in 2007 was an amnesty for illegal immigrants. He now says that he has realized the error of his ways on this issue. Let's hope he has, but we all know that the Democratic candidates will be infinitely worse on illegal immigration. This is especially true when we consider the fact that the Democratic Party will probably have a considerable majority in both houses of Congress come January 2009.

If Mrs. Clinton or Mr. Obama has their way we might have as many as forty million more citizens with the simple stroke of a pen.

One of the last considerations that I want to address in the presidential election of 2008 is the possibility of a third party candidate. Two people immediately come to mind when we look at the potential to have a third party candidacy: Mike Bloomberg and Ron Paul. It is very hard to assess just how Bloomberg may affect the race. In actuality he is a liberal, but he switched parties in order to run for the position of mayor of New York City. He went from Democrat to Republican, but has again switched and has become an independent. Ron Paul, on the other hand, will certainly take votes away from the Republican McCain. If this were to happen he will assuredly play the role of spoiler that Ross Perot and Ralph Nader did in the respective presidential elections in which they were involved.

We could go down the litany of all the major issues and contrast the positions of the Democratic candidates with McCain, but that would be essentially rewriting this book. I feel that the conservatives in this country have a choice: either the Senator from Arizona or a socialist. We can moan all we want about the fact that we don't believe Mr. McCain is conservative enough, but that won't change the reality of the choice that we have. In a two-party system it is either/or; in this case the hope that Hillary Clinton and Barack Obama never take the oath to sit in the Oval Office is all too clear. Four years of either of them could be tantamount to national suicide. God forbid eight!

ABORTION

The issue of abortion is clearly one of the most contentious in American political debate. It is intensely personal and touches upon so many of our fundamental belief systems. Few issues bring out feelings as strongly as this one does. The issues of life and death, freedom, and personal choice and accountability, all resonate fiercely when we address abortion. Very few things bring forth as much emotion in me as does this debate. To be honest, the fact that we even debate it is disturbing to me and what it means for our society as a whole.

Life begins at conception. When the sperm and egg come together they have a unique genetic code for someone who can exist. If that baby is carried to term it will emerge and start a new life in our world. I have a hard time listening to arguments that attempt to strip the fetus of its humanity. Even if it is just a bunch of cells they are human cells. What gives anyone the right to deny another their right to exist? I say this both morally and constitutionally. The only moral reason that this is acceptable is if the mother's life is threatened due to the pregnancy. Considering the Constitution we have to add cases of rape and incest where the woman did not choose to become pregnant, therefore having her rights violated.

Since 1973 we have outdone the Nazis' murder of about 16 million people by about three times. For a nation that says we have a right to life in our Constitution this is disgusting. I try not to personalize my beliefs when I am dealing with people who feel differently than I do, but it is not easy. Abortion is murder. When someone thinks that the deliberate extinguishing of an innocent human being is acceptable I am troubled by that thought. My experiences teaching in a high school have only served to deepen these convictions. Most of the abortions in this country are due to ignorance and poor choices. If you can't afford, or don't want, a child, then don't have sex! Isn't that simple enough? Isn't that obvious? If you make that mistake and find that you are going to be a parent shouldn't you then take responsibility for what you have done? I can't tell you how many times I have foregone having sex for these exact reasons.

When we debate this issue we often hear the liberals speak of choice. Yet, I say that this choice exists when people choose to have sex. This choice accounts for the vast majority of pregnancies. Why should an innocent unborn child die for the carelessness of its parents? This is the height of selfishness and irresponsibility. When worse comes to worst there is always the option of adoption. Isn't giving a child a chance at life better than snuffing it out before it has even had a chance to live? I know that there are not going to be enough adoptive parents to take on all the children born from unintended pregnancies, but this speaks to the idea of restraint and responsibility. If you don't want a kid, keep your legs closed and your zipper up and there won't be a problem.

We often hear talk of the viability of the fetus when it comes to abortion. Those who make this argument had better watch out because they are stepping onto a very slippery slope. I could make the case that significant portions of the adult population aren't viable. Would they be able to exist without the help and support of others? Would any of us be able to exist without the help and support of others? I think not. Viability does not determine whether one is human, our genes do. And, even then we have to consider the sanctity of life that God has bestowed on all his creatures, not just people. All life is sacred and this is an important part of this debate.

The quality of life of any unborn child is quite often pointed out as a reason for aborting it. I look at the next logical step in this argument: Is the pro-choice crowd contending that all people who are poor or uneducated should be murdered? Do they want to start a genocide in the slums and the third world to eliminate all those who do not have a stellar life? Will they next move onto every depressed teenager in the industrialized world who is dissatisfied with the current condition of their life? I know I'm being facetious, but these are the thoughts that are the next logical conclusions if you accept the first point. Life is not always easy. Many have had troubled upbringings and still found a way to make something of themselves. Is it not arrogant to presuppose that these children would be better off dead? I don't know about you, but I would rather be given a chance at life rather than being stopped before I ever even got a chance to get started!

The Constitution of the United States is unambiguous: we have a right to life. Should not the law put the burden of proof on those who want to deny this right to others? Clearly, the right of the mother, as a fully functioning human being, supersedes the right to the unborn, but that is only when her right to life is threatened. Yet, the classifications of what constitutes a threat to the mother's life have been greatly exaggerated. Headaches and vomiting are merely an ancillary part of pregnancy, but we have seen the left take these ordinary conditions into court and turn them into debilitating emergencies. Our law needs to center on the realities at hand, not the imagined or exacerbated claims of those who wish to abdicate the responsibilities of their own choices. A human being is a human being, whether or not they have already been born!

When I speak of the right to life on behalf of the unborn, I am speaking about the most innocent of us all. We are not talking about the right of some duly convicted murderer. We are speaking about someone who has just come into existence. They have had no chance to do wrong or harm to anyone. How can a society that prides itself on rights and freedom deny them a chance to live except under the most dire of circumstances? If we fail them I am sure that we will fail us all.

THE RIGHT TO BEAR ARMS

The Second Amendment to the United States Constitution is one of the most important rights that we have. Without the right to bear arms all of our other freedoms rest on the willingness of the government to allow us to have them. And that is antithetical to the originator of our rights in the Declaration of Independence, our creator. The ability of the government to supersede its authority is directly proportional to the rights of citizens to defend themselves. This is demonstrated throughout history and the founders understood the dangers of the state being the sole possessor of armed force. America's democracy has survived because the people have the right to keep and bear arms.

Obviously, this issue causes quite a debate between liberals and conservatives. Some of the issues are worthy of debate, but the extreme left attempts to use the wording of the amendment to deny that we as individuals have the right to possess firearms. They take the phrase "well-regulated militia" and attempt to suggest that this means only the government can maintain arms. Yet, this completely ignores the second part of this sentence which states that the "people" have this right. The left refuses to see the correlation between the right to bear arms and the ability of the citizens of this country to maintain all of their freedoms. They also refuse to accept the correlation between high crime rates and strict gun control.

According to the amendment the government has the right to regulate arms. It does not have the right to ban them altogether. It is interesting to note that the places with the highest gun-related crime are areas with the strictest gun control. Why is this the case? It is because criminals are the main cause of gun-related crime. When they are assured of unarmed victims they are free to pursue their illicit activities with peace of mind. When citizens are allowed to carry weapons they preserve the right to defend themselves and their fellow citizens. Could the Virginia Tech massacre have been as bad as it was if some of the other students had been allowed to be armed? Would the Holocaust have had as many victims if the people of Europe had had the same rights as Americans? Look at the final fight of the Jews in the Warsaw ghetto, when they finally did use arms to defend themselves, despite being woefully out-gunned. They didn't defeat the Nazis, but they sure took a hell of a lot with them.

Personally I don't own a firearm and probably never will. Yet, I count on the ability of my fellow citizens who do have arms to help defend me if the need ever arises. If we allow the liberals to disarm us then we will have no recourse to defend ourselves from criminals or from a government that may try to take away our rights. In order to maintain our freedom the Second Amendment is not only necessary, but vital. Look at how much undue power the federal government already exercises in this country. Could you imagine what the politicians would do if they knew that the population had no recourse to their accumulation of power?

Now we do have to look at the proper way in which regulations should be administered. It is also imperative to establish the legal and moral grounds that the government has on its ability to control arms. For the most part each state should maintain the right to make specific laws. Yet, we must move away from the near prohibition on arms that exists in many states and cities. This is especially true of the northeast part of the country. We must beware when gun control becomes an effective ban on gun ownership. Americans will not lose their rights quickly, but rather in increments. As few people as possible should be excluded from the right to bear arms.

What is the basis on which the government should be able to regulate arms? I think that basis can be found in the Constitution. Our system of government is founded on the belief that the government is there to protect our basic rights to life, liberty, and property. This essentially means that the regulation of arms should be based on the lives and safety of the citizens as a whole. This is why some of the more powerful weapons need to have much stricter control than small arms. Yet, we must not let the law over step its legitimate boundaries. Obviously, no one wants a neighbor with a nuclear weapon next door, but establishing the limit on how much firepower is too much is difficult. There are collectors and military historians that do have a use for some pretty unusual pieces of equipment. The best way to regulate this is to preserve the basic right, but to make the threshold for permits to such weapons as high as each community deems necessary while adhering to the Constitution. Punishment for breaking gun control laws should be very severe as well. This will ensure that responsible citizens do not suffer due to those who are irresponsible. Our behavior does reflect on our ability to exercise our rights.

Gun control advocates on the left like to conveniently forget the realities behind gun crime. All crimes are committed by those who do not follow the law. Somehow the liberals seem to believe that those who do not follow the law already will suddenly abide by a new more restrictive statute. Stiff penalties, for the use and transportation of illegal weapons, is the best way to combat the flow of weapons to criminals and gangs. Gun companies and dealers also need to make sure they do everything possible to prevent arms from falling into the wrong hands. The best way to combat crime is to go after the criminals, not the law-abiding citizens who have a right to defend themselves.

Americans who believe in the right to bear arms are considered to be peculiar by some of our neighbors around the world. This can be best explained by a story that I have that relates to this subject. I used to work at an office building. In the mid-1990s there used to be a British man who worked for a package delivery company. He and I used to talk politics all the time. We got along very well and had very good conversations together. One day the subject of the right to bear arms came up. He made an offhand remark to the effect that some Americans were gun nuts and that they were crazy when it came to this issue. He then said they think that the government may try to take their rights away some day and this was preposterous. When he finished he looked at me and could tell from the look on my face that I was just about to tell him that I was one of those people. He was astonished, because we usually agreed on most subjects. It was almost beyond his ability to believe that I could think such a scenario was possible. Yet, this tale demonstrates the fundamental difference between those who believe in the right to bear arms and those who don't. I don't trust the government to be the sole power with weapons, and I don't want to have to depend on the authorities to defend me in my time of need. I want to be able to defend myself by any means necessary!

Therefore, it is essential for Americans to be vigilant in maintaining our right to bear arms. We must maintain the ability to protect ourselves from criminals and to check the powers that be if the situation was ever to arise. The Second Amendment is not the product of a bygone age as the left may have you think. It is as necessary today as it was in 1791. I hope I will never have to use a weapon to defend myself, but I want to maintain the ability to do so if the time ever comes that I have to. Any attempt by the governments of the United States, or international bodies, to infringe on our right to keep and bear arms is a step toward tyranny. We fought a revolution to establish our rights endowed by our creator. It is we who allows the government to have rights, not the other way around.

ECONOMICS, TAXATION, AND SOCIAL SECURITY

These three issues are inextricably tied together, but I want to look at how they all are intertwined. The policies of the American federal government concerning these subjects is fast becoming a crisis. This is especially true of Social Security. Overall, our general economic welfare is not currently threatened, but this will not be the case over the course of the next few decades if something is not done immediately to start to address these major issues. All one has to do is take a glance at Western Europe to figure out what lies in store for an America unchanged. Slow economic growth rates and an inability to finance the retirement of the elderly are nearing an epidemic in Europe. We need to alter our system if we are to avoid a similar situation. Thank God we have avoided the socialism that has created their problems. Our inclination towards a more capitalistic economy has given us some breathing room to deal with these issues if we act now, but this will all fall apart if we elect people who use these failed European systems as a model on which to base our economy.

Capitalism, like democracy, is not a perfect system, but they are the best systems around. Government control leads to bureaucracy and bureaucrats are notoriously short-sighted and incompetent. Obviously, some regulation is necessary in any economy, but the question becomes, how much? There is a degree of variability in the answer to this question, but the best answer of all is as little as possible. How do we maintain the strong growth we have had over the last several decades and meet the challenge of paying for the retirement of the baby boom generation? We cannot solve this problem unless we integrate our current policies with how we meet the needs of the Social Security, Medicare, and Medicaid programs. For far too long politicians have avoided finding solutions to these issues, because the fact that any real means to address it will certainly cause some sacrifice of every member of our society. These fears of alienating large blocks of voters have effectively prevented any serious attempt at reform. Yet, if we do not address these problems we will only allow a more serious situation to evolve.

Any ideas I propose here will need to be polished if they are to be applied to the populace as a whole. Yet, I hope my suggestions can help in laying a foundation for the economic system we will have in the future. We need to maintain our vitality while allowing our government to meet the obligations it has promised in the past. Fostering the growth we have had in recent years will allow us more leeway in the mechanisms we use to pay for those who are retiring and to preserve the same benefits for the future of those who are in the workforce now. Failing to balance these disparate needs will only promote greater problems in the future. We can't rob the cradle of one generation to pay for another, and we cannot continue to pretend that these economic burdens won't eventually destroy the economy as a whole if left unchanged.

Maintaining the economic prosperity we generally enjoy is essential to solving the problems we face. If we were to undergo any calamity on this front it would diminish our abilities to deal with these issues overall. When this is considered we must find what those things are that make for a strong economy. Clearly this leads one to look at taxes. Liberals seem to think that the answer is to tax our way to be able to pay. Yet, this ignores the fundamental effects that taxes have on the economy. Higher taxes actually encourage individuals to hold onto the money that they already have, rather than invest it or start new businesses. Heavy taxation acts as a retardant to entrepreneurs. Why would anyone invest when the fruits of their labor will have to be doubled, or tripled in order to make any profit? Is it not better to sit on such assets rather than risk them on such tiresome pursuits? Why work to make a pittance when doing nothing gets you the same thing?

To those who do not study economics it may be counter-intuitive to realize that raising taxes in our current economy actually lowers the revenue that the government receives. Yet, this is exactly the case. The dramatic tax cuts enacted by Ronald Reagan in the 1980s increased the money that the federal government received, but a failure to reduce spending eventually led to deficits. Therefore, the model is simple: reduce taxes for all who pay and reduce the amount that the government spends. The former is easy; the latter has been a bane to the existence of politicians for time immemorial. Our current crop of politicians, both right and left, have spent our tax dollars like it was water and they have Niagara Falls in their pockets. Who knows how much we could save if we were to cut wasteful spending from our government budgets?

The premise that tax cuts help economies is quite obvious. Think logically and simply; consider how people react to any attempt to take their hard-earned cash. Most will skirt the letter of the law as closely is as legally possible. Others, who are less scrupulous, will do everything in their power to hold onto their income even if it means off-shore bank accounts and extremely creative accounting. When these barriers to the free movement of capital are removed all of this hidden money comes flooding back to the economy. When wealth is free to be invested and utilized, it has a snowball effect on the economy. Once clandestine dollars are put to work, people get jobs, they spend their money, more profit is secured and that is reinvested, starting the whole process all over again.

Let me give a case in point. How many people would think that one of the most vibrant economies in Europe is that of Ireland? I would hazard to say only those who study economics, yet this is actually the truth. For centuries the Irish were one of the poorest countries in Western Europe; now their per capita Gross Domestic Product is higher than that of Great Britain. How did they accomplish this? They lowered taxes on individuals and corporations and the industries of the world flocked to their country to reap the benefits. Conversely, we can look to the nation of France. They have hobbled their own indigenous investment with high taxation and discouraged international investment with the same. Only those who absolutely have to will do business in France; even many of its own people are looking to take their firms elsewhere. Maybe Sarkozy can put an end to this and reinvigorate their economy.

Taxes in the U.S. are low, but they can be even lower. Recent cuts have helped our economy stay afloat in rough times, yet we still have many immoral and regressive taxes inhibiting our people as individuals and the nation as a whole. Proposals to raise the tax on gasoline, or to maintain those that already exist, will harm the poorest amongst us the most. The wealthy are unaffected by such taxes while those taxes account for a considerable portion of the income of those less well off. The death tax, or the estate tax, is one of the most unjust of all. Here we have the government stepping in and essentially confiscating property that has already been taxed before. Why is it acceptable to force families to sell homes that they have had for generations to pay the greedy, wasteful government? Liberals will often point to the ultra-rich to justify these thefts, but they rarely discuss how this affects those in the middle class as well. Should the fruits of a lifetime of labor not be allowed to be passed onto one's own family, regardless of what class they are in? What gives the government the right to inheritance?

The liberals always go after Wall Street. They act as if the stock market and financial institutions are only there to service millionaires. This ignores the fact that more middle class Americans have money invested in the stock market than ever before. This is due to 401K plans, mutual funds, and online trading. It also ignores the fact that it is investment which begins the process of economic growth. All of the Democrats want to raise corporate taxes, dividend taxes, and the tax on capital gains. What will this do to the economy? It will cripple the will to invest, and if the will to invest is lost the entire economic engine loses the fuel that it needs to run. This will cause further erosion of jobs and wages, and this will hurt the lower and middle classes the most. There is no separation between the classes when it comes to taxation. Increase the burden for one group and all will end up suffering.

Completely unfettered capitalism has shown its problems in the past. Government regulation has its place, but it must not be a deterrent to economic growth. Child labor laws and safety regulations are two of the most reasonable regulations to point towards. I think that there are few who would want to allow our country to step back to where we were in the 19th century on these issues. Other, more modern regulations concerning industrial waste disposal and environmental impact usually fall into this common sense category as well. Yet, we have to watch how some of these "reasonable" regulations get implemented. Once the sticky hands of the government are involved in anything they are very hard to remove. Over-regulation can have the same effect on an economy as higher taxes.

We hear a lot these days about making moves to regulate the salaries and compensation of high-level executives in corporations. As nice as this may sound, it is a dangerous road to embark upon. I too am troubled by the near-exponential growth of the money being earned at the top levels of companies, compared to the average employees, but this is a situation that we are probably best off letting capitalism address. The inordinate change in executive compensation ultimately affects the bottom line performance of the companies who engage in these practices negatively. Investors will eventually react to these unnecessary expenditures and look for investments that do not waste money on salaries and bonuses that do not reflect the efforts of those receiving them. If the situation continues to spiral out of control then regulation may need to be considered.

The same method of addressing the problem needs to be used to curb the over-compensation that unions have engineered. Part of the reason that corporations are moving production abroad is the undue pay and benefits that are being given to employees. Retirement and healthcare insurance are bankrupting certain industries; this is especially true of manufacturing. How can companies pay people full benefits and pensions when they work less than twenty years, in some cases? Yet, just as in the case of the overpaid executives, we need to allow the capitalist system the chance to eradicate these problems. If the economic system can not do this in and of itself, we will continue to watch jobs move to China, India, and the third world as a whole. We will be left with only high-skill labor that cannot be exported, and this will not meet the employment needs of our population. Unions need to fight for just compensation for their members, not windfalls that bankrupt the companies employing them. Not only does this hurt the businesses, but eventually it hurts the workers.

Many new methods of taxation are also being explored by economists at this time. The system we have now is clearly odious, but I am skeptical of simply overturning overnight the way in which taxes are collected. Part of what attracted me to conservative principles is the idea of an organic society. This essentially means a gradual, well-thought out means to change most problems. The culture and institutions we have are the result of the growth of our past actions. I know that this complicates any move to make a drastic change in our tax system, but the possibility of catastrophic, unforeseen consequences is great. This does not mean that I am against these new plans, the foremost among them being the consumption and flat taxes, but only that I am extremely wary of the complete alteration of the system we have in one all-changing stroke.

Energy consumption will be dealt with in its own chapter, but I am impelled to mention it here. The hunt for alternative forms of energy production is one of the most important components of the functioning of our economy. If we should find an adequate source, or sources, of energy that would complement the energy we use today we could use the savings to improve our economy in ways we can only dream of. Personally, I think this could be the crucial piece of the puzzle that allows us to become independent of the tiresome imposition of other nations' influence on what we do here at home. Most Americans do not realize that if tar sand and oil shale are included in the figures that it is the United States that has the largest oil reserves in the world. Many of the globalists are interested in keeping these reserves untapped. Many of their tax and energy use policies are centered on just such a prohibition on the use of our own American natural resources. Furthermore, I await the day that more ingenious methods of energy production free us from the use of fossil fuels. Yet, until that time we must utilize the energy sources that we have at hand.

We can look to the Kyoto treaty to see how the globalists want to destroy our economy. The plan is to create a system of carbon emission caps. The plan sets the caps for industrialized nations low compared to what our economies already generate. Conversely, the treaty puts caps on developing nations inordinately high when compared to what they now produce. The hope is to create a carbon trading market that will have the wealthier nations buying carbon credits from the poorer nations. What this plan will effectively do is transfer money from the first world to the third world. It completely ignores the realities of moving our economy from one source of energy to a number of others. Yes, we should reduce the pollution we cause, but we should not enter into a false market that is designed to essentially be a socialist welfare system among nations. Kyoto, or anything like it, should not be apart of our nation's economic future.

The American economy has to maintain the jobs that we do have and move to create jobs for the future. Our high standard of living should make it abundantly clear that we cannot compete with the likes of China and India for comparable wages. The benefits that are necessary for American workers to survive make us uncompetitive with most of the rest of the workers of the world. The answer to this problem is simple: technology. The only way that the United States can maintain manufacturing is to utilize superior technology. Our citizens will benefit the most from instituting production that relies more on mechanization than manual labor.

It is imperative that we have a strong manufacturing component in our economy. Over the last several decades we have outsourced this critical element from within our borders. Not only is this naïve, but it is short-sighted. What will happen when we have lost the ability to produce for ourselves? Our country cannot afford to depend on foreign production to meet our needs, especially in times of war. This reliance allows our enemies and competitors to wield an inordinate amount of power on our foreign policies and defense. The basic reason that the United States played such a significant role in World War II was the incredible ability that we had to out-produce Germany and Japan. I fear that we no longer have that power. Therefore, I think we need to reinvigorate our manufacturing base and return as much of our potential to provide for ourselves as we can to within our own borders. Again, as is the case with almost everything, this is a process we must start now, but we must do it in a manner in which we allow our economy to adjust to change rather than be thrust into change. Industry is essential to our national defense. America should never depend on the rest of the world, but on our own abilities and God.

The most difficult economic problem to solve is the issue of entitlements. Like it or not, our government has promised Social Security, Medicare, and Medicaid. Left as the system exists today all of these programs will go bankrupt in our natural lifetimes. I know it may sound quaint, but a promise is a promise. Governments, like people, have the obligation to live up to the expectations that they have created.

Now, does this mean that the United States federal government is bound to destroy its fiscal solvency to meet its prior commitments? I say no! What it does mean is that we need to immediately address the very serious financial mess that our incompetent politicians have created. Dealing with these problems today is one of the most serious challenges that we face in maintaining our ability to have an economy that will be viable in the future.

Medicare and Medicaid are such cumbersome enigmas that I have to admit at this time I would have to study them far more in depth to even approach the means necessary to correct their faults. What I do know is that we have to trim the expenditures of these programs if we are going to be able to have a sound financial future. The odious regulations of these programs cause people to contort their financial positions into pretzels in order to get the help that they desire. Many elderly citizens sell off all of their financial holdings and possessions in order to qualify for these programs. The government should move to find ways for private medical insurance to become more competitive. This will reduce costs to the consumers and help alleviate the burdens that the uninsured place on the system. It also will help reduce the costs incurred by Medicare and Medicaid.

The problem of Social Security is a particular point of contention between the left and the right. When George Bush tried to address the issue, the Democrats categorically blocked his plan at every turn. The Democrats actually gave a standing ovation to themselves during one of the State of the Union addresses for their successful prevention of Bush's plan. Rather than come up with a plan of their own they simply opposed the president. Now, that's real leadership. If we are ever going to solve the problems with Social Security we are going to have to get beyond petty partisanship.

Although Bush's plan wasn't perfect it was a step in the right direction. Some form of privatization is the just thing to do. The government forces me to pay into Social Security, but there is no chance that the returns that Social Security will provide will match what I would have made had I been allowed to invest the money myself. A system needs to be designed that will allow people to start to privatize a portion of their Social Security taxes. The system should be tiered, based on age from retirement, and be grandfathered into existence. This way the government can adjust their payouts to the change in the funds they receive. A cap on the percentage of the tax one can divert into a private account would probably have to be set. The more one diverts into a personal plan will proportionally reduce the money they get from Social Security.

Obviously, I would like to opt out of Social Security completely. Yet, I don't think that the government can meet the obligations that they owe to retirees if we allow everyone the ability to stop paying into the program. So, the next best idea would be to let people gradually and partially leave the system. Too many citizens have come to depend on Social Security to be the source, or major component, of their retirement income. This is why we must change the program in a way that does not disrupt those who need Social Security. I especially believe this to be true because these people were forced to participate in the system. They cannot be faulted for what they did not choose to do.

It is noteworthy to point out that Congress does not participate in Social Security. The very people who want to keep the rest of us in a broken system have found a way out for themselves. This is so typical of our politicians in this country. What's good for us is not good enough for them. Social Security will be gone if nothing is done to change it before 2050. Some estimates put the bankruptcy of the program a number of years earlier than that. The federal government must stop spending the funds that are supposed to be marked for Social Security on other budgetary items. They also must allow people, like myself, the ability to at least partially opt out of the program.

The economy is a very complex subject. I have avoided spelling out all the specifics of the ideas that I have to improve the functioning of our economy if not only to prevent boredom, but an unnecessary exposition of tedious facts and figures. It is imperative that we get our government to act now. It is also important for the people of this country to recognize the fact that we will all have to sacrifice in order to meet the needs our economy will face in the future. Plans that attempt to put the burden on the upper class will only have a delayed detrimental affect for the lower and middle classes. This especially applies to taxation and Social Security. The economy reacts best when the rates are dropped on all citizens and corporations that pay taxes to the government. The stimulus of the Reagan tax cuts was repeated by the Bush tax cuts in the early 2000s. Too bad the overspending by the federal government was also repeated. The day our elected officials act with fiscal responsibility will be the day that our economy begins its march toward its true potential. As of now the government has always been a nagging restraint on our economic performance.

THE FAMILY IN SOCIETY

The greatest blessing that God has given me in my life is my family; not only my immediate family, but my extended family as well. The benefits that have come to me from being associated with my relatives are incalculable. I have had numerous role models, both male and female, that have taught me to be a good person and how to be successful. They have shown me through example and advice what it takes to face problems, disappointment, death, employment, relationships, and everyday life. I have been shown how to endure the hard times and how to enjoy the good. Yet, I know that this is not the case for far too many people in our society. Their experience has been the complete opposite. I know this not only from the media, but from my personal experience working at a Special Education high school and my personal life in general. Good families are an essential part of good cultures. I fear that America is becoming far too dysfunctional in our family life to be successful as a nation.

It is impossible assess the impact of detrimental family life on our society. How many of our problems can be traced back to broken homes and abuse that occurs among those who are supposed to care for us the most? Strong, loving families are the foundation for a strong culture. When children are neglected or harmed by those who are meant to love and nurture them, the damage to their psyches is often lifelong. The effects ripple through every relationship they have and their ability to function in society is inhibited in all the facets of their lives. Individuals who have experienced serious problems in their family interactions or who have been left to fend for themselves often are unable to form positive interpersonal relationships. These people then go out into the world with a social handicap that hinders their daily lives in every possible way. It's almost as if they have been confined to a social wheelchair.

I am not saying that those without strong, well-functioning families cannot be productive members of society, but only that they will typically have a harder time achieving success. We can tie many social problems to unstable and abusive family life. Increased drug and alcohol addiction, higher incarceration rates, prostitution, teen pregnancy, out-of-wedlock births, and a greater propensity to drop out of school are just a few of the more salient problems exacerbated by family dysfunction. Of course these problems happen even in ideal situations, but they are far more likely to occur when individuals don't have a good experience while growing up.

Part of our development as human beings is learning from others how to behave. Poor examples will often yield poor results. The first five years of life are essential in laying the foundation of what we become in adult life. I have seen personally the effect that abuse and neglect in those important years has caused. Some of my students have had learning disabilities and behavior problems that can be traced to the problems of their early lives. Many of these students will struggle the rest of their lives with low self-esteem, depression, sub-standard academic performance, and social pathologies. All of these factors serve to retard their ability to socialize and manage everyday tasks. This is especially true of those who have trouble reading, doing basic math, and those who are socially disabled from their experiences.

Abuse, regardless of the type, and neglect often yield the same result. Physical, mental, and sexual abuse are probably the most devastating incidents that can affect one's personality. Neglect leaves an individual with a weak foundation, both emotionally and socially. Individuals that have endured these difficulties often have trouble trusting other people. They also often have problems in their ability to have functioning relationships. These disabilities blunt the potential of those so affected to contribute to our society positively. In fact, they often lead to destructive anti-social behavior. Every person who does not live up to his or her full capability detracts from our nation as a whole. How much better would our country be if all citizens were given the full opportunity to do their best in life? Obviously, we will never achieve utopia, but we need to do better than we are doing right now.

A stable mother and father are clearly the ideal when it comes to parenting. We learn the roles that gender plays in our lives from those who are around us. Parents who love, nurture, and properly discipline their children permit for them to become better functioning adults. Children model the behavior that they see around them; the more stable and caring the environment the better chance for individuals to grow and perform at their full potential in society. When a person is lacking a strong role model from either sex it negatively affects their ability to socialize. When both a male and female parent is not available, the next best thing is to have someone close substitute in that role. Part of the problem we see with youth today can be seen from the fact that many young people have been left without a strong male figure in their lives. This leads to women who do not expect proper treatment from males in intimate relationships, and boys who model themselves after boys. I feel that much of the disrespect and objectification of women in our popular culture is derived from this lack of strong male role models.

Many of the problems that come from dysfunctional families are far more tangible. Students learn better when they have had the attention given to their basic skills. When parents interact with infants and toddlers they are establishing rudimentary abilities. Speech, reasoning, and perceptual skills are some of the more basics that are being absorbed. We also learn in those early years how to physically interact with other people and things. Over-protective parents can cause a child to be just as unready for the world as abusive or neglectful parents. Young people who have parents available to aid with homework and social activities are also given a better foundation on which to function. We need to teach children their basic skills at home before they ever set foot in a classroom.

This leads me to discipline. Whether one believes in spanking a child or not is irrelevant. What is most important is that a system of consistent correction and punishment is established. One should never threaten a child with a consequence that they know will never be able to be carried out. Punishment must also be consistent with the behavioral infraction incurred. Good parenting is doing what is in the interest of the child, not acting out of anger. I feel that the liberal tendency over the last several decades has been to reduce the effectiveness of parents to discipline their children. When I have students telling me that they will call DYFS (Division of Youth and Family Services, New Jersey's version of child protective services, and I use the term protective loosely) on their parents or guardians for legitimate disciplinary actions, it's clear that things have gone too far. It becomes even more apparent when the state agencies are actually taking action against parents who have done no wrong. A good child is one who has had behavioral boundaries clearly defined. Successful members of any society must know the limitations and expectations of the culture in which they exist.

Now the question becomes what role, if any, should our government play in ensuring that each child has the best possible family situation? This is a very tricky question to address. Obviously, preventing abuse is one function of the state, but what other involvement is in the overall interest of society? How does the government help foster better family circumstances? One thing that needs to be done is to make sure that all government programs and policies encourage stability and the closest thing to a nuclear family as possible. Many welfare programs penalize recipients when they get married. Personal finances are also often negatively affected when couples get married. Simple adjustments to certain government policies can go a long way in facilitating good family life. We also need to find a way to reward those people who become guardians in lieu of those who have failed to live up to their obligations as parents. Whether this is someone who adopts, or someone who is a relative, it needs to be recognized that their sacrifice is helping the society at large.

I feel public ad campaigns are essentially useless. If someone taking care of a child doesn't know where the kid is at ten o'clock at night, I doubt a television commercial will teach them proper parenting skills. I do believe, however, that part of our health education programs should have a component that centers on the responsibilities of raising a child. Too many guardians do not know how to provide for a child's physical, social, educational, financial, and spiritual needs. Our education system should be able to help impart some of these basic skills of parenting. Remember the concept of modeling: If one generation is dysfunctional it usually passes those dysfunctional habits on to the next generation. This then becomes a cycle that spirals each successive generation a bit further down in their ability to raise children to be stable, productive members of society.

It is difficult to gauge just how much our nation is adversely affected by dysfunctional families. Those on the left who decry the family as a patriarchal institution are idiots. A strong family is the best way to produce strong individuals in our society. Trying to replace the family with the state is one of the last things we should be trying to do. Learning through experience what it means to be a well-adjusted human being is essential to our development. The best tool that we have to engineer this proper development is the family. When an ideal situation is not possible then those involved must do the best that they can with what is available to them. And for those who have not had the best experience in their upbringing, may they do their best to provide a good life to the next generation. Strong, loving families are the best foundation on which to build a strong, well-functioning society.

GENERAL FOREIGN POLICY

I often hear it said that Osama Bin Laden would not have worked with Saddam Hussein because Osama is fanatically religious and Saddam was a secularist. This is a fundamental misunderstanding of the manner in which geopolitics is carried out. The world was stunned in August 1939 when Hitler and Stalin announced their regimes' mutual non-aggression pact. It had been assumed that the fascist Nazis would never work with the Soviet Communists. Yet, these ideological enemies saw the advantage of working together, even if only for a short time. This reality must be applied to the international stage as it exists today. "Nations don't have friends, they have interests." We must not make assumptions that the enemies of this country, and the Western world as a whole, will not defer their deeply held beliefs in order to gain an advantage in their conflict with us. To do this is not only foolish, but it could be extremely costly in lives and finances.

When looking at foreign policy in general we have to not only look at potential conflicts, but how we deal with the developing world and the relationships we have with allies and other major powers such as China and Russia. Issues of trade, the environment, development, aid, and relations with the other significant powers must be considered all together. We learned from our abandonment of Afghanistan to the Taliban that the world cannot allow a safe haven for fanatics. By the same token we cannot allow the third world to remain in a state of poverty and perpetual warfare. If we do it will only be a matter of time until these problems affect us here at home. Prosperity for the world as a whole is essential for prosperity in the Western world.

We must also not make the mistake of believing the first world can solve all problems by providing aid to the developing world. We need to find the methods that will allow their economies to develop their own self-sustainability. Aid is only a temporary solution to these problems. South America poses a number of concerns, much of Asia still needs significant improvement, and Africa is a complete disaster. The developed nations need to work more diligently to address the issues that face our less affluent neighbors. Yet, we see little cooperation among the major powers, and over the last several years we have seen the return to agitation between the interests of these nations. Russia is actively helping Iran in its development of nuclear power, China is increasingly and alarmingly building a formidable military, and many of the people of Western Europe perceive the U.S. as a force of evil in the world.

The European Union and the capitalist powers of the Pacific Rim do much to aid the third world. Yet, when action beyond charity is needed they essentially abdicate their responsibility to America. The Chinese and Russians are so absorbed in the development of their own economies and interests that they only get involved with foreign aid when it suits their plans. The situation in the Sudan exemplifies this. The reason that the U.N. has done nothing about the Darfur genocide is that the Chinese have an interest in the oil produced by this nation. Even if the U.N. were to react, it would fail to use the force necessary to address the conflict. The world body refuses to even use the term genocide when it comes to Darfur. What else should we call the massacre of hundreds of thousands and the displacement of millions? The failure of the other major capitalist powers to address conflict situations in the developing world is becoming an increasing problem. The U.S. is already committed to a series of military engagements and police actions. We cannot continue to be the sole police officer in the world. Western Europeans can trace their timidity to combat to WWI. The Japanese have been almost pacifistic since their extreme outburst of violence in the 1930s and 1940s, and the South Koreans have their own problems with the North. Outside of small contingents of troops sent by other nations the U.S. has almost been left alone to deal with international conflicts.

It is not possible to clear the world of tyranny. It is also not the responsibility of the United States to put an end to every petty dictatorship that arises on the planet, but it should be the goal of our foreign policy to inhibit these despots from functioning with ease and impunity. Sanctions and the support of opposition to these regimes should be an integral component of how we project onto the world stage. It is unrealistic to think that we can topple every regime that does not respect human rights. Yet, when we do, such as the cases of Afghanistan and Iraq, it is important for us to understand the necessity of helping that nation repair the damages from conflict and to assist them in establishing a stable government. To do any less is not only immoral, but presents the possibility of the same destabilizing conditions being recreated.

Corruption in the governing bodies of the third world allows for many of the causes of extreme poverty. It is the failure of those in charge who are to blame for the wretched conditions faced by billions around the globe. Yes, I understand that the forces of colonialism and imperialism helped create the situations in many of these nations, but most of them have had several decades to bring their countries into the modern world. In most cases they have failed miserably. To continue to pour aid into these money pits is no longer an option. All foreign aid should be tied to a comprehensive plan for its use and what happens with the funds should be transparent. These conditions are entirely reasonable. The U.S. sends billions of dollars abroad every year and, simply put, we are not getting our money's worth in return. In many cases the people of these nations hate us. I will go as far as to say that it is necessary for us to tie aid to the support of our policies and interests. This does not mean I expect these foreign governments to bow to our every whim, but that if they oppose us continually then it is not in our interest to continue with any assistance programs.

Infrastructure is the key to any improvement in the third world. Electricity, access to water, transportation systems, and sewage disposal are probably the most important to the development of any nation. Many countries are held back by their inability to provide these basic needs. Healthcare issues stem from the lack of these necessities. Millions live in absolute filth. This causes disease and inhibits the economic growth so vital to ending poverty. Aiding countries that make efforts to improve their infrastructure should be a priority in our foreign policy. How many great minds are being lost to the destitute conditions that exist in so much of the world? Modernization is essential to help lift people out of the cycles of poverty.

Education is also very important. Too many of the world's children are not receiving a proper education. When people are unable to read or write their ability to know about the greater world around them is limited. The understanding of what is happening around the globe is essential to forming an opinion on what must happen locally. How many people live their whole lives not knowing that what they experience does not have to be? How many people also do not have an adequate understanding of what their neighbors around the planet are actually like? It is this ignorance of other cultures that permits for so much hatred in the world. Obviously, we all will not always get along, but the potential for humans to relate to one another greatly quells the propensity towards conflict. The teaching of daily living skills could also improve the unsanitary conditions that exist in too many places. Programs like the Peace Corps can be an essential means of providing help to the unfortunate and a line of communication between those in need and those who have.

Disease is a major problem in the developing world. AIDS is especially devastating in Africa. Many of the countries in southern Africa have average life spans in the thirties. These nations can never step into the twenty-first century if few ever live to have enough experience to know how to solve the problems that they face. Other diseases also inhibit the ability of people to claw their way out of poverty. Cholera, typhoid, malaria, and diphtheria are just a few of the perennial illnesses that destroy lives throughout the developing world. The industrial nations must do what we can to help alleviate the cost of disease in poorer countries. Providing for vaccinations is just one step that we can take. Providing volunteer medical professionals from the developed world, and education programs that allow for citizens from the developing world to study in our countries' universities, is just a start.

While focusing on the third world it is important to consider the need for international efforts to cooperate on environmental issues. Most of the tropical forests on the planet are in developing nations. These forests are essentially the lungs of the world. The loss of these eco-systems is not only a danger to the countries in which they exist, but to the world as a whole. Our policies should foster the preservation of these habitats. In order to do this alternative economic pursuits must be found for those who live in these sensitive areas. The industrial nations also need to change the way in which we use the resources that come from the developing world. Forests are just one of the topics on which we need to cooperate. The issues of over-fishing in the oceans, species preservation, agricultural impact on the land, and the prevention of pandemic pathogens from developing are just a few of the other salient issues that need international cooperation.

Trade is the lifeblood of the world economy. The Great Depression was caused in part by a worldwide trade war. Numerous nations enacted protectionist policies that discouraged international trade. The lesson learned from that is that trade needs to be as free as possible. Breaking down international impediments to free trade is in the interest of all involved. I don't like seeing jobs being siphoned off to China and India, but putting up unnatural barriers to the freedom of corporations to do what is in their interest can have catastrophic effects that can be far worse than the loss of employment in the developed world. We need to combat job losses here with innovation, not protectionist policies. Are there certain circumstances that may warrant some form of protection for indigenous economies? Yes, but they are few and far between. We need to respond to these difficulties by increasing our production capabilities, not by artificially erecting barriers to trade.

America has dug itself into a deep hole. We are continually borrowing money from abroad to finance our consumption of goods produced overseas. This is especially true of China. If Americans want to reduce our trade deficits and our borrowing then individuals need to change their buying habits. If Americans want to stop the loss of manufacturing jobs to foreign countries we will have to bite the bullet and pay more for goods that are produced here. Even if we make technological developments that increase our output of goods it will be a while before we see the benefits from any such policies. Developed nations can change their stance in the world economy if they want to. All they have to do is create as much of the goods that are used in their economy at home. The only caveat is that they will then have to bare the higher cost of paying workers from an industrialized country.

I believe that most people would like to have input into how they are governed, but it must be realized that not all people think that democracy is as great as those in the West do. In many nations there are higher considerations in the minds of the population. Many religious people in certain regions of the world would prefer a theocracy. Others believe that stability is the most important component of governing. We have to be cautious when we try to place our values onto others. What we see as a fundamental right, such as religious freedom, may be seen as an imposition by other people. We also have to be wary that we do not see our form of democracy as the only one. How many differing forms of republics do we see in the developed world? Each nation has evolved a system that suits the conditions in its own society. We must allow this to occur in the rest of the world as well, but this does not mean we cannot assist in what they create if they want the assistance that we offer.

One of the most significant foreign policy issues of our time is nuclear proliferation. This especially is true of Iran, North Korea, and Pakistan. These three nations pose specific problems that none of the other nuclear powers pose. Iran is a theocratic state that has repeatedly threatened Israel and the West as a whole. It might also pass nuclear weapons off to terrorists if the situation were right. North Korea is run by an unpredictable madman who will not only use nukes, but may sell them to the highest bidder as well. Pakistan is now run by a dictator who is working with the West because it suits his agenda. What will happen if Musharraf no longer sees his interest in working with us? Or worse yet, what would happen if the radical elements in Pakistani society or their intelligence agencies were to gain control of the reins of power? Nuclear weapons do not have to be carried by missiles; they can be detonated very simply in the form of a dirty bomb. Yes, their true power lies in their ability to be used in atomic chain reactions, but they can have a devastating effect with the simple combination of fissile material and explosives. The current path of negotiation and sanctions should be continued, but we have to think about the possibility of further actions if these softer methods do not yield the results we desire.

I think that the United States has had an overall positive effect on the history of the world, despite all of our faults and mistakes. We need to continue to be a force for good in the world. Yet, we must realize the limits that any one power may have on the world stage. I do not care about the public opinion polls in foreign nations. I do not want to subject our country to the power of international bodies. Yet, I do think we need to be a positive national citizen in the world. America has been blessed by God. We need to remember this when we step onto the international stage. We must not be arrogant, but we also must not allow ourselves to be reduced to a position that is less than what we have earned. The United States of America is a great military, cultural, political, social, and economic power. We did not get this way by worrying about our perception in the rest of the world. We must do what we are inclined to do and hope that the world community will eventually see that we have had the best of intentions in our actions. And if they don't, I really don't care. We have to participate in the affairs of the world without looking over our shoulders.

The world is in a very bad place right now. I hate to say it, but I foresee conflicts that will make WWII look like a quarrel. The forces of evil are gathering their strength. All that is good in the human race is being turned over on its head. Mankind is heading for a series of events that will threaten our very existence. We are threatened by changes in the environment, social pressures, and the political competitions that exist between so many varying powers. I would love to be positive and say that I think that the human race will come together and meet these challenges, but I am hard-pressed to see this course of events. Yet, I will not lament. I will do all that I can to try to bring about the changes that we need to make it through these most serious times. Never in the history of man have so many forces been stacked against our survival. May God give us guidance, perseverance, and strength!

FEMINISM

This issue divides liberals from conservatives in a number of ways. The left will contest that they are the only feminists. They routinely try to fashion the idea that the right is for the oppression of women. They continually point to Roe vs. Wade as a victory for women, claiming it finally allowed women the right to control their own bodies. Time and again we hear the mantras such as, "I am woman, hear me roar" or "If a man can do it women can do it better." Despite such simplistic reasoning pertaining to the roles of the sexes these notions have had a great impact on our society. On one hand we have seen the removal of many impediments to the achievements of women and obviously that has been good. On the other hand we have seen the demasculinization of our culture and the confusion of gender. Men need to be allowed to be men and women should be allowed to be women. We are equal in our rights, but we are not identical in our biology.

It must first be noted that there are no concrete definitions as to what makes a man and what makes a woman, except our biology. Yet, it is fair to say that there are archetypes that we do associate with either gender. Unfortunately, radical feminism has come to identify men with all that is wrong in our society. Testosterone has become synonymous with brutality and violence. Men have been associated with base and animal impulse. The lifting up of women has become identified with the belittling of masculinity. The simplistic notion that if women were to ascend to the reins that control our society somehow we would enter into a new utopian age has become a part of our cultural psyche. Not only is this erroneous, but it ignores the synergy that has existed between the sexes throughout all cultures, places, and times. Yes, men have had the preponderance of power in society, but they have not fashioned the world without the participation of women.

Men are not inherently bad, neither are women inherently good. Switch the gender and the same can be said again. I have often heard those on the left claim that Judeo-Christianity encourages the oppression of women. This shows a great misunderstanding of the tenets of those two religions. Many from this point of view see Eve as the antagonist in the story of the fall of mankind from grace. In actuality, both Adam and Eve are the cause of the fall of man. Evil is the true culprit in the story. Eve trusts the serpent over Adam, and Adam chooses to listen to Eve instead of God. The story is not meant to blame either sex for the sins of mankind, but to exemplify the necessity of people to follow the will of God. "In Christ there is neither Greek nor Jew, slave nor free, man nor woman." Failing to understand the equality that God has given us is a fundamental misconception of the word of the Bible.

I believe that men and women were made to complement each other. How this has been turned into the ludicrous definitions that many have of what is a man or what is a woman is beyond me. No one should be confined to a narrow understanding of our gender roles. Over the course of time women have been denied their rightful place in society. Yet, much has been done to remedy this over the last several decades. Instead of demonizing men we need to look at what will bring about the opening of opportunity to women in general. Universities, board rooms, and political positions have all been brought into the realms of possibility for women. Is further advancement desirable? Yes, but we must not artificially put people into places in society. Ensuring that the laws are fair and equitable will allow for the natural empowerment of women in the 21st century.

Some of the issues that concern the fair treatment of women are legitimate. Women earn less than 80% of what men earn for comparable jobs. Some of this disparity can be explained by pregnancy and family leave, but that should not constitute the difference that currently exists. I do not believe that we can legislate absolute equality. Society must grow out of the sexist notions and beliefs that it has succumbed to over very long periods of time. Unfortunately, I feel that there is little to be done except to await the infiltration of the ideas of equality to work their way into the psyches of society. The best way to encourage this is for individuals to challenge stereotyping and discrimination when they encounter it. Other than that the law can be applied when oppressive actions are so egregious that there is no way to deny there illegality. Examples of this can be found in sexual harassment and when a particular organization has established a record of suppressing the advancement of women.

As I write this we are currently engrossed in the presidential elections. For the first time we are seeing the real possibility that a woman could be elected to the highest office in our land. Yet, we hear some say that America is not ready for a woman president. I will speak for myself here. I'm ready for a woman—I just don't want it to be Hillary Clinton. Her destructive policies would be just as dangerous were they to be articulated by a man. I could accept a Thatcher or a Golda Meir, but Hillary has nothing to offer except for socialism and capitulation on the international stage.

One of the issues most associated with feminism is the issue of abortion. The liberals like to portray this as the right of women to do as they choose with their own bodies. I have no problem with that argument except that it ignores the fact that the rights of another body are at stake in this case. Roe vs. Wade is not about the right of a woman to control her own body; it is actually about the right of women to abdicate the responsibilities of having sex. Their right to control their own bodies came when they had the choice to have sex. When they engage in sex they are allowing for the possibility that they will become pregnant.

Once they put themselves into this position it is their responsibility to do all that they can to bring this new life into the world. How many of us are rightfully disgusted by pregnant women who continue to drink or smoke cigarettes? This is because common sense dictates that these actions are adversely affecting the most innocent of us all. Rape and incest are obvious exceptions to this line of thinking.

Many on the side of the radical feminists rail against the traditional family as a patriarchal institution. This notion strikes me as a perversion of what the family is supposed to be about. We all know that the established culture of the 1950s pushed the idea of a strong, controlling father figure. It was exemplified in the popular culture of the time and has had a significant impact on the mentality of our society ever since. Despite these unfortunate portrayals of the family this is not the reality in the vast majority of homes. Families need to have both a strong male figure as well as a strong female figure. Children need to have examples to follow from both genders. There is a male and female component to all of our personalities. Failing to have strong figures representing both sexes in our developing years retards our full and complete growth into functioning adults. Good families are not patriarchal; they are an example of what strong human beings can be regardless of sex.

One of the greatest failings of our culture is the objectification of women. I must admit that the beauty of a woman is matched by little in the universe, but that is only a surface feature of those particular individuals who possess these features. Never should the looks of a person be an overriding factor in how they are perceived. Yet, our society has come to utilize these images to sell products, grab our attention, and value the worth of a woman on her physical appearance. This is a major contributor to eating disorders and mental illnesses in the females within our society. It also harms the men of our culture when the salient features that they appreciate in a woman are all superficial. Sadly, I think to some degree women have fallen victim to the same objectification of men over the past few decades. People in general need to be recognized for the qualities of character that they live and breathe every day. To do anything less is to miss the souls that God has put into each of us.

I want all of the people of our society to have the potential to be what they can. To belittle women is to belittle about half of our population. We can not afford to lose or inhibit any of the talents that members of our culture possess. No one should be held back by anything other than their own failures to succeed. Our society is both masculine and feminine. Both sexes have a great deal to offer to our advancement as a whole. Pitting the sexes into a pitched battle only detracts from our abilities to benefit our nation. A great America is a nation of both strong men and strong women.

JUDGES, THE COURTS, AND JUSTICE

The justice system in the United States is far from perfect, but it is one of the best in the world. Some of the problems that we have in our courts are endemic to human nature while others are a product of our own particular failings. Our system is overworked and over utilized. The courts are inundated with unnecessary cases and often times the judges themselves are hampered by the restraints placed on them by the law. The issues in our halls of justice can be best remedied with common sense. The problem with that is politicians and lawyers have too much say into how are system is run. Yet, these are the very people who we need to address the problems that we face.

Our justice system is like a garden that has been left untended. It's had enough rain to grow, but all the good plants are being choked out by the weeds. What we need to do to restore the garden to its verdant potential is clean out all of the unwanted growth. Once the weeds are taken out all of our plants will be able to thrive and produce flowers and vegetables. Our system hasn't been weeded in generations. Our garden is overcrowded and barely productive. It's time to get our hands dirty and restore it to the purposes it is intended for.

Despite my imperfect analogy my point is obvious: we need to clean the garbage out of our justice system. Too many cases are brought before our courts that can be settled by other means. Also, the great length of many cases has become a hindrance to the operations of our legal system. In many areas of the country they are setting up alternatives to the court system for more minor offenses. This idea needs to be explored in much greater depth.

Our society has grown to be extremely litigious and I do not believe that it is helpful to our nation. How much of our time and energy is wasted on cases that have no business going before the justice system?

The United States has more people per capita in jail than almost any other nation in the world. This is largely due to the fact that we send people to jail for offenses that do not warrant it, and in many other cases the amount of time given for sentences is way over what it should be. Ironically it is the criminals who should be locked up that seem to be given the most leeway in this country. Truly dangerous violent criminals are sentenced lightly compared to those imprisoned for fraud, theft, and tax evasion. What we need to do is have a system that has the punishment fit the crime. We also need to allow judges more leeway in the handling of cases. Part of the problem with our system is the difficulty of writing laws in and of itself. It is very hard to codify in language the common sense we need to apply to specific cases. Mandatory sentencing reduces the ability of our judges to apply insight and perspective into the situations brought before their respective benches. In some cases the laws are too broadly applied in others they are not applied harshly enough it is the magistrates that are supposed to correct this inherent flaw in human law. The way the system works now we have essentially stripped the judges of this part of their duty.

One of the biggest problems in our justice system is the specter of illegal drugs. I have to say that I do not have very concrete answers on what to do about this, but it is clear that the illegal nature of many narcotics increases their price and fuels a vast underground economy and culture. This underground culture is often violent and is the root cause of many of the problems that we face in this nation. The cost in lives to innocent people and law enforcement agents is incalculable. The cost of fighting this illegal trade is also exorbitant. The criminal activity fed by this voracious monster has consumed good portions of our youth for generations. If we could reduce or eliminate this source of financing for the criminal organizations that utilize it we could possibly destroy these enterprises.

The hard part in this equation is figuring out how to best accomplish the partial or total decriminalization of drugs. In the case we have today we cannot use the example of the prohibition of alcohol. Drugs are too diverse compared to liquor and some have such horrible side affects that it is right to question whether they should be legal in any way. Yet, the system as it stands now is completely overwhelmed by illegal drugs. In many cases these drugs are used to bankroll criminal cartels and even terrorists. The allure of easy money also seduces far too many of our young people. Plus, the illegality only fosters a culture of disrespect toward the law. The easy part is to say that we need to change the way our justice system handles illegal drugs; the hard part is figuring out how. Rather than attack this problem in depth I feel it is best at this time to simply throw the possibility out there for debate. Many have had good ideas on how to handle this problem and what problems would come from changing the system that we currently have.

Let's take a look at a different issue in our justice system, the appointment of judges and justices. Over the last two presidential terms this problem has grown into an all-out war between the liberals and the conservatives. The days when nominees were approved with a minimum of political bickering are over. Yes, there were cases in the past that were contentious, but the problem now is that virtually every appointment is challenged with the utmost hostility. This has gotten so bad that many courts have not had any judges approved to fill vacancies. We already have a backup in the courts as it is without having the partisan politicization of the process. As much as I may hate to say it, largely because there is the chance that we may get a Democratic president in 2009, the appointment of judges by any administration should only be blocked if the candidate is unfit for office in some manner. This does not include not liking their politics.

Part of the problem that we now have is that the left and the right are even starting to divide on how they view law. Liberals take an activist approach to interpreting law and the conservatives believe that we must use the strict construction of the law as intended by our founders. Now, this delineation can be met with some partisanship on my part, but I want to point out some of the characteristics that separate the two ideologies on this point. Conservatives believe that the U.S. Constitution should be the sole arbiter of the interpretation of law in this country. Many liberals have been looking to international and foreign law to justify their legal opinions. This has been evidenced in many of the opinions handed down by the leftist justices on the Supreme Court over the last several years. The federal Constitution should suffice to define the laws that we have in our nation. America is a truly unique country and using foreign law to interpret our statutes is unconscionable. Apply this line of thinking to our Second Amendment and it would disappear in the liberal seas of Western Europe or the United Nations.

One of the most important jobs that our next president will have is the picking of one or possibly two new Supreme Court justices over the next four years. This will sway the balance of the court regardless of the partisan nature of the president. Over the course of the next several years many cases that will define our nation for decades shall come before the highest court in our land. Many other cases, almost as important, will come before the lower district courts as well. The next president will have the chance to shape the nature of this country quite significantly. Hopefully, we will end up with justices that use our Constitution to interpret the laws in the United States; otherwise I fear we may get stuck with the likes of Ginsburg, Souter, or Stevens.

One idea that has been thrown around about our Supreme Court has been the consideration of term limits. Some have even suggested that we elect justices, but that would be a mistake of an incredible magnitude. The main reason for appointing Supreme Court justices to life term was so that they did not have to take politics into account in their decisions. In fact, it is in the best interest of the law to entirely remove the role of partisanship from the court. Yet, electing justices would have just that effect. Term limits on the other hand may reduce the undue influence that these nine people have come to have on our culture, justice system, and laws. Since 1973 only twelve years have been under Democratic presidents, yet the Supreme Court has been decidedly liberal in that time frame. We may need to look at the possibility of ten, twenty, or thirty years on the bench as being an adequate stay on the highest court in the land, but this would take a Constitutional Amendment.

Historically, our justice system has been a fair barometer of where the nation stood socially. This has not always had favorable results. For nearly eighty years the courts not only upheld but expanded the institution of slavery. The court reaffirmed the legality of second class citizenship in Plessy vs. Ferguson, which upheld the legality of segregation. Yet, as much as it offends our sensibilities today, these decisions reflected the culture of their time. Despite my many disagreements with the decisions of the courts over the last several decades I feel that they too do represent the culture of our time. I say this considering decisions such as Roe vs. Wade, and Kelo vs. New London. Yes, these cases represent our culture, but it just happens to be a culture that I don't want to be part of. I hope that Senator McCain will be the next president so that we can see a court that begins to reflect the subculture that has grown in size and force in this nation, the conservative movement. It is a culture that respects life, approaches matters on the world stage in the realms of reality rather than theory, and allows for individuals to have the most freedom when it comes to utilizing the talents and strengths that God gave them. Much like the universe, if the liberals continue to expand and expand the construct of the law eventually it will lose all relevance. And much like the universe, all matters will be but independent particles floating freely in the netherworld of space, unable to contact or influence one another.

If our nation is to survive this liberal onslaught we will have to change the types of thought that have come to represent our justice system over the last fifty years.

America has a good but imperfect legal system. We have seen the evolution of our justice system over the two-and-a-quarter centuries that our nation has existed. We have grown to accept many different peoples and ideas into our notions of law over that time. The beauty of what was set out by our founders is the potential for each generation to modify the laws of this land overtime. The problem with this system has been the potential for each generation to modify the laws of this land overtime. I fear where we may go if we have the liberals of this generation appoint the judges and justices that will shape our nation for decades to come. Yet, if that is the will of the people I just might have to stand by and clench my teeth. At worst that will only last a number of decades or so. Que sera sera!

RELIGION AND THE PUBLIC SPHERE

This is an issue in which I take special interest. The very foundation of who I am and what I believe is my faith. Without God nothing would exist! All other issues are intertwined with religion. I understand that in society we have to permit for freedom of belief, but that does not translate into the removal of religion from the public sphere. In fact, it proves that religion must be allowed in the public sphere because it is the right of individuals to choose what they believe in order to be free. In order to be free people must be able to express themselves in public honestly and unfettered. America is based on the idea that, "All men are created equal, that they are endowed by their Creator with certain unalienable Rights." These rights are the basis for the permission of religion in our public life.

Let's be clear: religion in America is under attack. The secular left prides itself on the prohibition of religious freedom. Under the guise of minority rights they are pushing for the complete and total removal of religion from American public society. Attempts to remove the words "under God" from the Pledge of Allegiance and the plethora of cases about religion in the public realm are just the tip of the iceberg. It is not enough for these people to be able to believe, or not believe, what they want, but it has become their mission to be insulated from the mere mention of religious belief. They are particularly belligerent towards Christianity and Judaism.

One of the greatest misunderstandings about the governing of the United States is that there is a constitutional separation of church and state. One hears this repeated ad nauseam in this debate. What the Constitution actually says in the first amendment is that, "Congress shall make no law respecting the establishment of religion, or prohibiting the free exercise thereof." The founders were not trying to make a religion-free society, but a government that was not a proponent of any one faith over another. If they were trying to make any mention of God an anathema in America, why does the Constitution contain the words, "In the year of our Lord"? Why was the rotunda of the Supreme Court decorated with the words of the Ten Commandments? I am not making the case that our founders were all religious, quite the contrary, but that they were not attempting to create a religion-free state.

No person in this country is persecuted into believing a particular religion. The government is not in the business of being a proponent of any specific faith. In actuality the government is exceptionally secular. In the few places religion is intertwined with government nobody is forced to participate. Nobody is jailed, prohibited from public office, or harassed by public officials for their belief or lack thereof. In fact if they are it is illegal and this rarely ever occurs. Yet, it is the extreme on the left that looks to establish its religion, agnosticism and atheism. Their attempt to totally remove any mention of God, or religion, from government facilities and public schools is the effective establishment of agnosticism and atheism as the official religion of the United States. Not only was this not the intent of our founders, but is unconstitutional as well.

The basis of all our law in the Western world is Judeo-Christian. The foundations of our social customs and societal mores are Judeo-Christian. The attempt to find other sources for the origin of our culture is pointless and disingenuous. If the left is unhappy with where we come from they should plainly state it. Instead we see twisted scholarship trying to find some new origin for our traditional values. We hear the constant denials that our founders looked to the teachings of the Bible on which to base our law, regardless if they were adherents to the religion. All this is intended to do is to further erode the place of religion in our society. This is part of their overall strategy to alter our culture and mold it into the shape of the world they envision, a world with no moral standards that accepts every vice, perversion, and affront to God as a virtue.

This move to take religion out of our society can even be found in something as mundane as historical dating. I don't remember when I first saw it, but I'm referring to the use of the terms B.C.E. and C.E. to replace B.C. and A.D. The new terms are supposed to be abbreviations for "before the common era" and "common era." I believe this is some ridiculous attempt to assuage those who have had their sensibilities offended by the inference that the life and teachings of Jesus were a turning point in the Western world. Yet, we must ask what this system is based on. Is it based on the common acceptance of a dating system about two thousand years ago, or is it still based on the approximate birth of Christ? Exactly like the tally of years we use today. Maybe they can find some other pivotal point in history more to their liking, possibly the birth of Darwin or Freud. These new terms are used on television and even in many of our textbooks in schools. When such radical ideas so easily work their way into our culture we begin to see the insidious nature of this liberal beast.

Occasionally, we see the right on the wrong side of this issue. This was the case when newly elected Congressman, Keith Ellison, was to be sworn in as part of the tradition of taking his position. Apparently Mr. Ellison, a Muslim, wanted to use a Q'ran instead of a Bible when they had a reenactment of the official ceremony. For some strange reason this caused a controversy. Several members of the conservative establishment thought his choice of the Q'ran was an affront to the traditions of the United States. I take exactly the opposite position. The Congressman not only has the right to use the holy book of his religion, but I would expect him to do so. True religious freedom is extended to all faiths. In fact, it must also be extended to those without any belief as well. That was the essence of what our founders were looking to create when they added the First Amendment to the Constitution.

Another area where we see the debate of religion in the public sphere is the issue of holiday decorations on public property and schools. This is another case where the so-called politically correct, or, as I like to call them, the politically wrong, have overextended their reach. It's one thing to have sensitivity to those in groups that are not so numerous, it is quite another to let a small percentage of people dictate what we as a society do as a whole. No less, when most of the people in those groups voice no objection to what the society as a whole is practicing. It is no surprise that our founders were more concerned with the tyranny of the minority than they were with the tyranny of the majority. If you don't believe me read the Federalist Papers.

I personally find this a strange point for me to defend because I do not use any decorations in my own home and probably never will, unless I marry a woman who would like to celebrate the seasons in such a way. Anyway I digress. It does offend me when businesses, schools, and public spaces are forbidden to say "Merry Christmas," or they fear putting up Chanukah decorations because a few cantankerous souls may complain that they are not all-inclusive. All-inclusive implies including all. Prohibiting the celebration of any holiday or festivity due to the annoying whining of a few is not what America was founded on. Quite the opposite, it is what makes us great. Rather than protest would it not be better to try to have the customs and practices of our more newly arrived neighbors included in our public spheres? Is something not usually better than nothing? Wouldn't the inclusion of varying religions and beliefs better help us to understand what is at the heart of one another? Yet it is not inclusion that the liberals are after, but exclusion!

The real purpose of these complaints and legal battles is not to bring a new openness to our society, but the hope that they can change the traditions and customs that have unified us in the past. I don't expect Muslims and Hindus to celebrate Christian and Jewish holidays, but rather that we all learn about what each of our cultures finds to be a reason to celebrate. For those who have no religious beliefs, they can choose to participate or ignore these festivities. No one was promised a country in 1776 they would always approve of, or that they would be comfortable in every moment of their lives.

The break typically taken in late December and early January in our school systems is the Christmas and New Year break, not the holiday break. When schools have off for Yom Kippur it is because the school system has decided that the Jewish component of the community is significant enough to recognize this day as a holiday. I expect this tendency to increase in respect to other groups as their populations rise in the United States. Obviously, with greater diversity we will not be able to take off for every day deemed special, because eventually just about every day will have some importance to someone. But we can allow communities to respond to the needs of the more numerous groups and accommodate those that are only represented by a few. Democracy is compromise, not absolute equality.

This now takes me to the use of the public square. All religious items that the general community finds acceptable should be allowed to be included. Symbols of varied faiths and cultures should have access to common space. Each season can have its differing decorations from the members of our localities. It is sad, but here I have to throw out the idea that perverted or grotesque displays might have to be excluded. We don't want to have a replica of an Aztec human sacrifice placed on the town hall lawn, or the figurines gracing the entrance to the local courthouse from some sex cult touting the virtues of the goddess Diana. When I speak of using the public sphere I refer to those cultures that are based on the similar goodwill and peace toward mankind that we hope our society is founded upon.

Now I want to look at a public space in which I have had quite a bit of experience, the schools. I cannot tell you how many times in my history classes that I have had a student tell me, "You can't talk about God in school!" I can't tell you how many times I have told them that one can talk about religion in historical and personal terms, but that one is not allowed to preach a religion or determine someone's grade based upon religion. This scenario exemplifies exactly what is going wrong in America. Young people have been so indoctrinated in leftist drivel that they think speaking of God in a public school is illegal. This mindset is not a mistake; it is exactly what the liberals are trying to inculcate into our culture. They are hoping to make people afraid to even speak the word God.

I find the issue of religion in public schools particularly interesting when the teaching of certain sciences is considered. The current state of affairs is completely in the control of the liberals. The theory of evolution, and mind you it is still a theory, is given the position of infallibility. Any attempt to question this idea is met with the most ardent opposition. It is also attacked with the most vicious campaign of distortions and lies intended to skew the perception of anyone who proposes a theory that challenges their precious evolution. Why? Because evolution helps to foster the idea that there is no power greater than the will of man in the universe. Their secular religions, atheism and agnosticism, cannot exist without a creation myth, and evolution is that myth.

In actuality, I tend to think that the general ideas of evolution are true. Yet, it is the supposition that life arose as the mere product of chemical interactions alone that I scientifically disagree with. Eventually I hope to write a book on the subject itself, but here I will have to keep myself within the constraints of religion in the public sphere. The consistent attempts of liberals to portray anyone who dares to want to discuss alternate theories to evolution as creationist whackos shows the house of cards upon which their explanation of how life came into existence is built upon. If their thoughts on the issue were so unassailable why wouldn't they welcome the debate and discussion that other theories would generate? Science and religion are not at odds with one another when one actually understands the ways in which nature and man operate. Using the Bible or the Hindu Vedas in science class is wrong, but examining the idea that life is far too complex to be a simple accumulation of interactions is scientific. One can debate how the process of evolution exists and what is the driving force behind it without leaving the confines of the scientific disciplines.

The secular world and the religious world do not need to be compartmentalized. America was found on religious freedom, not freedom from religion. All people have the right in this country to decide what it is they believe for themselves. We also have the right to express those thoughts in the public sphere. When communities choose to display the beliefs that its members hold dear they should not have to meet a standard that permits for the offense of no one. Freedom comes with the fact that sometimes we may not always like what others express. Life in a democracy cannot be lived if all people all the time never have to see or hear ideas that are different from their own, even if that means someone may have to hear the word God.

ENERGY

Energy is going to be one of the greatest challenges in the 21st century. The conservation of fuels that we already use will be important, as well as the development of new sources of power. Society can not function without energy and the methods we currently use are finite. As the population of the world grows we are going to have to meet the needs of billions more people. The potential catastrophes that await the people of this planet if we do not diversify our energy production are almost unimaginable. Civil unrest, wars, and famine will be the result if we fail to change now. Every energy source has its benefits and detractions balancing these two disparate forces should be the main focus of how we change our energy policies. Not only is this important for the world, but it is an important consideration in our national defense. America cannot allow itself to remain dependent on foreign sources of energy. To do so is to subject ourselves to the whims and events of a very unstable world.

The first place that we need to look when considering energy is to fossil fuels, in particular oil. There is no realistic possibility that we will switch to alternative energy overnight. We need to approach any changes in policy with the idea that we will have to wean ourselves from oil onto other sources of energy. Yet, we cannot take an approach that is lethargic. We must not shock our economy, but we do need to aggressively address this issue. The sooner we start, the less painful the experience will be. It would also be prudent to remember that most of the developing nations of the world will not be able to adjust as quickly as the first world, and in actuality it is most likely that they will increase their use of oil before they reduce it. I feel that some sort of international cooperation is necessary, but every attempt that has been made in this arena has had the tendency toward socialism and the strong flavors of anti-capitalism and anti-Western venom, the Kyoto Treaty probably being the best example of this.

Recently, oil crossed the hundred dollar a barrel mark. This is largely due to the near exponential rise in demand from nations such as China and India. These two countries represent about one-third of the world's population, yet they are only in the incipient stages of modernizing their economies. The ideal way of handling their increase of energy use would be to have them utilize as many alternative sources of energy as possible at the onset. The problem is that they must be willing to do this. This challenge is especially difficult when it comes to the Chinese. The Communist state has shown little inclination toward anything other than the rapid expansion of its economy. Their increase of the use of CFCs in the past proves that they cannot be relied on when it comes to this issue unless there is a significant change in the attitude of their leaders.

The rise in oil prices has an inevitable ripple affect throughout the economy. This is especially true of low-end consumer goods. This essentially means that the preponderance of the pain in personal budgets hits the lower and middle class the hardest. All products that need to be transported have a corresponding increase in their prices. This ripple affect has become readily apparent to anyone that has entered into a grocery store over the past several years. The only way to combat this inflation is to reduce the demand for oil. This can be done in two ways: increase the production of oil or find other sources of energy. This is basic economics, but the methods of doing this are extremely complex. I also think that simply increasing the amount of crude sucked from the earth is only a temporary fix at best. This is notably disconcerting when we consider that emissions from fossil fuels are the main source of atmospheric pollution.

When oil shale and tar sand are considered, the U.S. might have the largest reserves of oil in the world. Rather than waste this precious commodity on the world markets today we should hold onto as much of it as possible for the future. It is safe to say that fossil fuels will play a role in the economy of the world for the foreseeable future. The current policies of the United States have left a considerable portion of our oil reserves untapped. The Gulf of Mexico, the Atlantic and Pacific seaboards, and the north of Alaska still have vast reservoirs of crude that remain virtually untapped. Holding onto these reserves would be prudent for the future; if we were ever to be engaged in a major conflict it would be essential to maintain the ability to produce all of our energy needs. We need to develop alternative sources of energy, but until they are working effectively in the economy we must keep the options that we currently have available. Today the main option is oil.

Two nations exemplify the move to alternative energy. One is Iceland; the other is Brazil. Iceland, due to its small size and population, can teach us, but the lessons we can learn are not necessarily relevant to a nation of our size. Brazil, on the other hand, is significant enough in terms of population and landmass that we can extrapolate a lot from their experience. When the oil shocks of the 1970s occurred Brazil began its move to alternative fuels. They have concentrated on using bio-diesel and ethanol. The change has made them energy independent, but it has caused some new problems. One of them is that the emissions from these fuels has led to nitric acid in the atmosphere. We have sulfuric acid problems from our own emissions. Brazil's independence is notable, but we have to investigate how similar changes would affect our economy and environment.

The island nation of Iceland has quite a different experience to share. The nation is essentially the product of the forces of plate tectonics. It sits over one of the more active volcanic areas of the world. This provides a significant amount of geothermal energy. The people of this country have done an excellent job of turning this heat into power. The best part of their efforts is that the pollution from such energy production is negligible. The problem is that the same potential for power does not exist in every part of the planet. Clearly these techniques should be utilized where they can, but the rest of the world will have to find other sources of energy.

Let us apply the Brazil experience to the United States. In recent years we have seen the move to increase our use of ethanol. This has had both problems and benefits. The problem rests largely in the amount of energy needed to produce the fuel. Currently it is about as energy-efficient as oil. It also has just about the same amount of polluting emissions as gasoline. These inefficiencies can be remedied, but thus far this has not become a reality. Since corn has been the main source for our ethanol it has also had a dramatic effect on the economy, not only on our nation but on countries that rely on our exports. We can diversify our sources for ethanol to combat this inadequacy, but the same result will occur if we rely on one plant. Ethanol should play a role in our energy production, but it is not the answer to our needs.

The best answer to this problem is energy diversity. We have to utilize as many methods as possible in order to minimize the pollution from any one source. There are a number of possibilities that need to be considered. Yet, there is one that I feel is far too dangerous to use, and that is nuclear power. I often hear people suggest this as the main alternative fuel. I think that this would be a grave mistake. The risks from its radioactive waste are extreme. It also poses a significant risk in terms of systemic failures like Chernobyl or Three Mile Island. Tell me when has mankind ever made a machine with which he has not had an accident? The rewards from nuclear power could be great, but its potential for disaster is just too high.

A number of energy sources exist in the natural world. Chief among these are solar, wind, geothermal, and hydro powers. Each of these can be harnessed in different ways and they all offer the potential for energy with little resulting pollution. Producing electricity and heating from these sources is probably the best possible way we can use them. By doing this we could also potentially power fuel cells that would be used for vehicles. As the infrastructure exists today most of our electricity is produced from plants run on fossil fuels. This negates the efficacy of fuel cells and batteries that are charged from these sources for electric. Yet, if we were to power our homes and businesses with these natural sources of energy we would greatly reduce our reliance on oil and coal.

Think about the incredible amount of energy that exists in the natural world. Our planet is heated from the sun, the wind blows across the land and seas perpetually, and water is always moving. This is not to mention the incredible forces at work in the Earth itself, the movement of tectonic plates, the release of heat from the Earth, and volcanic activity. Finding ways to capture these natural forces could greatly facilitate our production of energy. Yet, the problem with many of these sources is our ability to capture them. Rivers can move turbines that produce electricity and we can use the actions of tidal forces in some places, but the transmission of that energy is the challenge. Solar power is exceptional, but there we have the waste from the panels and mechanisms that harvest this energy. Wind power is abundant, but how much of the planet do we want to cover with massive wind turbines? Geologic forces can provide a great deal of power, but they are somewhat limited by our proximity to these sources.

Vast quantities of methane also exist on earth. Yet, it too has its potential problems. It will produce emissions that will lead to some atmospheric pollution. This does not negate its use, but it does mitigate it. Realizing the use of methane also poses problems in how we access it. Much of the reserves of this gas are currently locked beneath the oceans. We must attempt to understand what, if any role, it plays in the eco-systems of which it is a part. Again, similar to ethanol, this can play a role in our energy production but it is not the sole answer to our needs.

Bio-diesel is an interesting concept. It can also be produced in a variety of methods. Harvesting fuel from the natural decomposition processes of animal waste and the decay of plant material are the two basic means of securing this power. Yet, it too releases emissions into the atmosphere that are not desirable. One of the best potential uses of bio-diesel is the powering of vehicles. Many of the solar and earth born energies pose great difficulties in their application to autos. Since automobiles are one of our chief sources of pollution anything that will reduce their emissions needs to be investigated intensively. Further research into the broader application of bio-diesel is absolutely essential.

Fossil fuels can be burned far more efficiently that they are today. Creating vehicles that utilize these commodities more effectively would be wise. The good news is that this is already being done on a significant scale. It is in the economic interest of the automobile manufacturers, both here and abroad, to make products that the consumers need. With the high cost of oil this means vehicles that can get the most miles per gallon. Though I do approve of this market force the recent artificial CAFÉ standards approved by Congress go too far. Science does not move forward or yield results due to the impositions by politicians in Washington. Clean coal can also be used in power plants. Despite that I do not believe this to be an answer to our energy problem, it should be used as an interim alternative. Fossil fuels that produce less emissions are better than their dirtier ancestors.

Fuel cells and batteries also have great potential. One of the bigger concerns, especially with batteries, is their reliance on heavy metals. One of the greater challenges in this field is to find more efficient sources of power and better ways of recycling or disposing of the spent batteries. Fuel cells are a bit more diverse. Some still have this same problem, but others rely on more efficient and less hazardous materials to produce energy. In some of the more innovative technologies air is used to create power, but this technology is still in its infancy. Together these technologies could possibly be coupled with energy produced from natural sources so that they gain their power from renewable and perpetual forces.

One of the more interesting sources for energy is nano-technology. This too is a new and innovative science. It also has a vast array of energy production methods, and I believe that we have just touched upon the tip of the iceberg. Nano essentially means small or microscopic forces. This can mean anything from miniature machines to the application of physics and chemistry to molecular and atomic processes. The field of nano-technology is wide open; it is also exceptionally diverse. Yet, it is a very poorly understood discipline of science. Its practical application could be just around the corner or possibly decades or centuries away. Nonetheless this is one of the options that could offer incredible amounts of energy with very little in terms of pollution.

One source of energy that I do not hear a lot about is magnetics. How many millions of people have ridden on trains that are powered by such technology? The forces of magnetics offer a clean source of energy. Yet, we see very little in its practical application. I have to admit that I do not know why this is the case. Almost everyone has played around with magnets at one point in their life. Virtually everyone knows the natural repellent force between similarly charged magnets and the attractive power of combining opposites. This form of energy should have innumerable applications that can use it. Perhaps further inquiry into this potential source of power is necessary.

Alas, the dream source of power. I have already ruled out nuclear power as it currently exists from my alternative sources of energy. Yet, that is only because we now use what is essentially a hot power with the potential for extreme reactions. The dream of scientists in this field is to produce what is known as cold fusion. This would essentially be the production of power similar to that which goes on in the sun.

The sun continually fuses hydrogen atoms into helium. When this occurs the latent energy left behind causes radiation. The dream is to fuse hydrogen atoms without the volatility that it typically yields, but the processes by which this can be done are beyond elusive at this point.

One of the greatest advances in the technology of mankind was the Manhattan Project. This was the program that the U.S. government implemented to develop the atomic bombs. Some project based on the similar coordination of scientific engineering and public funding would greatly advance our move to alternative sources of energy. In this case it would not have to be a clandestine program, so funds could be provided in more innovative ways. The state and federal governments already invest some tax money in this area, but this alone will not suffice. Raising taxes is not an option because it will only add to the stresses that the economy is currently enduring. Therefore other means of funding such a project would be necessary. Tax breaks for both research and results would be most desirable. The specifics of any such program would need to be worked out by the government and the companies and research facilities involved. Result-oriented incentives can be based on the percentage of what any fuel reduces our dependency on foreign oil. We would have to be careful that such a project did not become a lumbering beast. I greatly fear involving the government in anything. Yet, this issue is so essential to the future of this country and mankind as a whole that it may be necessary to take such a step.

One last consideration is the behavior of individuals. The simple things like recycling, turning off lights, and reducing our use of energy as a whole is important. The actions of one person are negligible, but when billions act responsibly and reduce unnecessary consumption the impact is magnified multiple times. I see so much opportunity to reduce waste in my daily life that I find this to be an important component of what we can do to minimize our use of energy. We don't need laws on this matter, but what we do need is to educate ourselves to how we can best utilize the energy we consume. The lives of every person on the planet are dependent on the power we use. From heating our homes, to transportation, to our use of electricity we are constantly consuming energy. It is about time that we begin to more efficiently use and produce that energy. The best means by which we will effectively change our energy production will come in a plethora of ways. Diversifying this production must begin now. Every region of our country and world need to implement the measures that best suit their economies and way of life. The international community should work together where we can, but we need to fight any plan that is premised on socialism and anti-Western concepts.

WHEN SECULARISM AND RELATIVISM GO TOO FAR

Both secularism and relativism have a place, but as usual it is those on the far left who want to take these ideological constructs too far. These ideas have applications that are completely legitimate. Yet, they become destructive to society when they are applied more broadly than is necessary. Secularism plays a role as a watchdog preventing the implementation of specific religious ideas into our government. This job has been virtually negligible over the last several decades. In fact, it has been legitimate expressions of religion that have been under attack in the public sphere. As for relativism, in its simplest form all ideas are perceived by the particular views that individuals hold. Yet, this becomes a problem when viewpoints are posited as fact. Secularism and relativism become dangerous when they are used as a hammer to smash our traditional culture and beliefs by the liberal fascists.

One of the primary differences between the left and the right is how they view truth. To the conservatives truth is an objective force. To the liberal truth is subjective. This may not seem like it is so important until one applies it to morality and society. When relativism is used to define culture all things become permissible. When truth is subjective there is no foundation upon which society can be built or stand upon. This is the true danger of relativism and secularism. How often do we hear that the Constitution is a living, breathing document? Yes, it can be changed, but only by the amendment process which was deliberately designed to be extremely difficult to do. The liberals have usurped this process and now use the courts to redefine the laws of this country by judicial fiat.

Secularism in its original form is the concept that no one religious system be established in the laws of our nation. It was meant to protect those who either do not have religious beliefs or those who are members of religious minorities. It was also meant to keep tax dollars out of religious institutions. Secularism in the form the left is currently trying to apply it has come to mean freedom from religion. When we see other Western nations passing laws that make it illegal for someone to say that they do not think homosexuality is moral we know that this ideal is being taken to an extreme. How are such laws not a violation of the freedom of speech for those who believe such things? How is it not a violation of their freedom of religion? Will we soon have laws that forbid people from stating that they believe abortion is murder? Secularism is supposed to secure the rights of individuals to determine their personal religious view. We have not had any real danger of the government establishing a religion in a very long time. The main threat we face today is the establishment of atheism and agnosticism as the de facto religion of the United States.

Some on the left in many Western nations are using the concepts of relativism in some very strange ways. Some of the more extreme are attempting to use this concept to overturn our society and traditions. We already see the effects on our laws governing marriage and abortion. We now see it being used to stop the assimilation of specific immigrants into our culture. Rather than encourage those who have come to our countries to adopt our culture we are altering our society to accommodate them. This has never been done in the past and will only serve to create a fractured nation that will end up in the Balkanization of the Western world. This problem is particularly apparent when one considers language.

In order for society to function, citizens need to have a common bond. We have that in our laws, concepts of equality, and our language. America will cease to be America if we continue to aid people in living here without learning our language. Schools should be a place where our children are taught the values and mores of our culture. We have to permit for some leeway in the participation of individuals, but we cannot have separate school systems for those of every subculture in our country. If people want to raise their children in the traditions and language of another nation then they can do this at home or in private schools. American public schools need to be based on the culture, traditions, and language that are the foundation of this country. Education fails students who are not prepared to be members of the society that we live in.

This problem can be seen in the religious accommodations that some are trying to push onto American society. Jews have always been a part of our national fabric. Even with some of their differing rules about conduct and diet they have managed to integrate into our culture and maintain their personal identity. Yet, we now are seeing a growing number of incidents where companies and individuals are pressing for religious accommodations that go beyond what we should accept. There have been cases when Muslim taxi drivers have refused to take lone women in their cabs, travel with alcohol, or take passengers that have been drinking. Cashiers of the Muslim faith have also refused to scan pork products. Truly this is their right as individuals, but then they need to get a different job. Any Christian that takes the Sabbath day seriously needs to find a job that does not include work on Sunday. In another case a corporation has banned pork products from the workplace. This was even carried to the point where individuals could not bring their own food if it had these products in it. When people have strict religious customs it is their responsibility to adapt to society, not society's responsibility to adapt to them.

It's ironic that the liberals push so hard for the inclusion of religion in our culture when it is not Jewish or Christian. On one hand they rail against any mention of God, but then turn around and push for classes that teach about Islamic faith and culture. Eastern religions are also part of the classes offered at most universities, but mention our Judeo-Christian roots and somehow this is perceived as exclusionary. Personally, as a historian I feel there is a great value in studying all of the cosmologies that our world has had. The more we know about past and present cultures the more we know about what makes human beings think, act, and live.

Another glaring example of this relativism is the refusal of many on the left to use the term terrorist. We often hear the saying one man's terrorist is another man's freedom fighter. And even though this is true we need to call the people who attack us terrorists; if we don't then is it not implied that one feels they are justified in their war against the West. When members of our own society can't even bring themselves to call our enemies what they are, we then have to ask what that means about how they view our culture and their personal place in it. Never before in the history of this country has so much sympathy been shown towards those we are fighting. Some on the very far left carry this relativism to the point where they are indifferent to our success in this conflict or even hostile toward our victory.

Applying relativism to the cultures of the world is a double-edged sword. On one hand it is the right of other nations to create the type of society that they see fit; on the other hand we need to lead by example when it comes to the rights we believe are endowed by our creator. Many nations around the world have citizens who, if given the chance, would elect to have a system based on religious law or a form of totalitarianism. We have to accept their right to choose such systems so long as they do not violate human rights or attempt to attack our society. The people of Iraq voted overwhelmingly to establish their country as an Islamic state. We need to respect their choice on this matter. Most Russians approve of the accumulation of power that Vladimir Putin has brought back to his position as head of state. Self-determination does not always mean a democracy as most Westerners typically understand it to exist. Yet, we should not tacitly approve of systems that use their power to abuse the rights of their citizens.

Let us take a look at relativism in its most extreme form. According to the relativists all cultures are equally founded on their own constructs of morality. When this idea is applied to the different societies of the world all things become moral. Relativists do not see the evil in human sacrifice. Relativists do not see the oppression of women as anything other than custom. Relativists believe that truth and morality are in the eye of the beholder. In fact this ideal can be carried so far that all things, no matter how antithetical to our own cultural ideals, can be accepted as someone else's truth. Most people who espouse these ideas are not always conscious of how far these thoughts can be taken. When truth is subjective, evil ceases to be evil. We cannot have justice in a society that has no basis to determine what is wrong or right. This pattern of thinking ends up in nihilism. All will tend to the destruction of society when we refuse to have even basic rules that apply to all citizens equally.

Secularism has its place when it is used to maintain the freedom of individuals to believe in what they wish. Relativism is good when it allows for people to understand the differing bases we have for viewing our world. Yet, both of these ideas are being carried into territory that borders on the insane. The foundation of our culture is being eroded by this tide relativism and secularism. Both are used to alter our society and change the traditional values that have made us what we are. When everything is reduced to perception then everything becomes acceptable. America and the West as a whole cannot be all things to all people. We must by definition have a culture that is founded on something. Those values are the sanctity of life, the concept that our rights are given by our creator, and that the freedom of every individual to pursue opportunities and their talents must be restricted as little as possible. America is the land of liberty not of license. Our laws must be based on these ideals if our society is to survive.

REBUILDING AFTER NATURAL DISASTERS

This chapter may seem insensitive to some, but this is a serious issue. We have faced a number of major natural disasters over the last several years from Hurricane Katrina to the California wildfires. The cost of rebuilding after these disasters has been exorbitant. In the future we may face more numerous and far more catastrophic events. It is imperative for our nation to look at the places and methods that we choose to rebuild. Unfortunately, in the immediate aftermath of any disaster we all have emotional blinders on. To add to this problem of truly investigating the wisdom of rebuilding we inevitably have the politicians descending upon any area that has been devastated, pledging billions to restore the affected region to what it once was. I know that Americans are inclined to assist those in need, but we have to start asking the right questions when it comes to rebuilding in certain places.

The first time I ever thought about the wisdom of federal assistance for those affected by a natural disaster was when I was on a trip to China. One of the families that were on the tour with me was from North Carolina. As we spoke, the fact that I chased hurricanes became a topic. While discussing this, the father of that family began to tell me his story of owning a beach house on the outer banks. For those not familiar with the region, the outer banks are the barrier islands of North Carolina. This area of the state juts out into the Atlantic in quite a prominent way. As we spoke, he told me that his house had been destroyed twice by hurricanes. What caught my ear was the fact that he said that the federal government was now paying for the rebuilding of his home for the second time. I wondered why this was the case since I, only a novice in the realms of climatology, recognized that the chances of his home being struck by another hurricane in the next decade was almost a certainty. I also wondered why the federal government would be involved in financing the rebuilding of an individual's home. He told me that they were not only rebuilding his home, but essentially the entire area that had been ravaged by this most recent hurricane. With this thought I began to ponder the prudence of building in an area that is so precariously poised on the brink of destruction. I would never buy a house in such a place and I wanted to know why the government was subsidizing the people who had chosen to do so. I have no problem with those who wish to engender such a risk, but why should the rest of the nation be forced to pay for such an obvious folly?

This is a question that needs to be asked in a variety of circumstances. How many of these areas are threatened with the near certainty of natural disasters? How far apart are the occurrences of these disasters, and what can be done to prevent them? If the answer is that there is little that can be done then we have to ask the next logical question: Should we be spending federal tax dollars on rebuilding and maintaining a community that we know is destined to be destroyed again? I believe that the answer is no. Those who wish to take these risks are the people who should bear the financial burden. If they continue to have a residence in these areas then it is their responsibility to accept the insurance that will cover them under these circumstances. To do anything else is to throw money at a problem we know will manifest itself in the near future.

We see this pattern repeated again and again, from the coasts of Florida to the canyons of California. Individuals want to live in these areas of pastoral beauty, but they are offered the potential to offset the cost of imminent disaster by the federal government. How many of these people could afford or would want to take the risk of the destruction of their property if they were not given this safety valve to their liability? I firmly believe that many of these homes and businesses would not have been built or been acquired had the government not permitted for the bailout once disaster appears. We need to discourage the development of regions that are subject to the inevitable forces of nature. It is one thing to face the forces of nature in general; it is quite another to brazenly build in areas that are destined for annihilation.

If one pays any attention to the forces of the weather and climate, it is readily apparent which areas we need to avoid when building. Obviously, we can not vacate these areas in totality, but we need to better address how we occupy such regions. I would like to look at some of the more vulnerable localities when it comes to natural disasters. Several regions of the country should suffice to exemplify the challenges that we face when considering this problem. Several types of natural disasters will also illuminate what threats are the most serious and frequent. I am not proposing that we abandon large tracts of land to return to the wild, but what I am suggesting is that we more intelligently allocate our resources when it comes to dealing with the forces of nature.

Most people do not realize that the most significant damage, in terms of lives and dollars, from natural disasters is due to flooding. Flooding is also one of the most prevalent forces of nature that mankind must contend with. Wherever we find rivers we find flooding. Wherever we find mankind we find rivers. Yet, we need to apply some common sense as to where we build. My home state of New Jersey offers some insight into this issue. Large parts of the northern part of the state are extensive flood plains. In our densely populated state many have homes in these areas. Originally, many of these communities were used for vacation homes during the summer, but as time went on and our rivers became polluted they were turned into year-round residences. Almost every town in the region has some part of it that is subject to frequent floods. Some places are so susceptible to these inundations that it is said if someone spits in the river they end up under water. All exaggerations aside, we have a significant portion of the people in this part of the state that live in areas that should never have been occupied in the first place. The conundrum presented to us is how to best extricate ourselves from this incessant flooding. The erratic weather over the last decade has exacerbated the problem because some places are flooding on an almost annual basis. Unfortunately, similar situations face us across almost the entire nation.

The opposite problem of wildfires exists primarily out west. Fire is part of the eco-systems in the western United States, but for decades the policies of government agencies was to suppress all wildfires. The result was an incredible buildup of dead plant material, which has become the fuel for the intense conflagrations that have plagued the western states over the last decade or so. Localities that endure fire on a sporadic basis are legitimate places to build, but areas that are reduced to ash every few years are not practical places to make our homes.

Hurricanes are also frequent visitors to the Atlantic and Gulf coasts of the United States. This is especially true of portions of Louisiana, Florida, and North Carolina. Obviously, we cannot abandon these vast areas of the country, but we do have to look to the practicality of the federal government providing insurance to those who build there. As I have already mentioned, some people are having their homes rebuilt for the second time, in some cases in less than a decade. The New Orleans area poses a special problem in this debate. The city is founded on land that was naturally replenished by the silt that came with the annual flood of the Mississippi River. When people occupied the land they cordoned the river off with levies and other earthworks to prevent the flooding of the city. This caused the silt to flow out into the Gulf of Mexico and the land has been sinking ever since. After a few centuries some parts of this metropolis are as much as fifteen feet below sea level. After the Katrina disaster the kneejerk reaction was to automatically say that we should rebuild the entire city. As nice as that gesture is, it is not practical. Spending billions on rebuilding an area that is destined to be inundated again is not the answer. If we are to put efforts into recreating New Orleans we must first raise the areas to at least five feet above sea level, make a Dutch-style levy system, or move areas of the city to places that are already above sea level. New Orleans is a historic part of our culture and character. I want it back almost as much as anyone else, but we have to look at the practical means of refurbishing the entire metropolitan area. Throwing billions of dollars into rebuilding a city that we know will be subject to disaster in the near future is not only foolish, but it will only allow us to repeat the tragedy and mental anguish that was endured from Katrina.

In the northeast of the U.S. we are frequently hit by Nor'easters. These storms can dump heavy rain and snow on our region for much of the year. They also have a tendency to cause extensive beach erosion. Year after year we spend incredible amounts of time, money, and energy into replenishing our beaches. In many cases luxury homes are built on the shoreline itself. Whenever these storms hit every major metropolitan region in the northeast has its specific locations that we send our news reporters so that they can watch beach houses crumble into the sea. Yet, year after year these homes are rebuilt as if this phenomenon won't occur again. In many cases state and federal dollars are used for this rebuilding. I ask, is this a good use of our tax payers' money? Or is it just plain stupid?

I've mentioned natural disasters that I do believe we can adjust to, but there are a few that we just have to accept and endure. Tsunamis, tornados, and earthquakes are catastrophes that can affect untold portions of this country. Each of these events can strike almost anywhere and at almost anytime. Tornados are very localized, but they can hit nearly every portion of our nation. Tsunamis are endemic to our coastlines, but they can strike thousands of miles of shoreline at any one time. Earthquakes essentially have no limit to their potential to affect America and their devastation can be minimal to catastrophic. We would have to abandon the planet to protect ourselves from these particular phenomena. So, I feel there is little to do when we choose where to build when we consider these particular disasters.

One of the best answers to dealing with natural disasters is to try to put some sort of limit on how we spend tax dollars on rebuilding. Maybe we could use federal insurance in less profligate manners. Assisting in rebuilding once, within, say, a twenty-year time frame, may be a potential answer to the problem. After this it must be up to the individual property and business owners to find private insurance. If they can incur the cost and the risk, then it is their personal choice to do so. The nation as a whole needs to stop throwing cash at regions that are perpetually assaulted by nature. It doesn't take a genius to figure out if an area is not a good place to build our lives and communities. America needs to stop wasting its efforts on the folly of combating nature, because when one chooses to fight nature it is always a losing battle.

POPULAR CULTURE AND THE MIND

I don't really know if popular culture is an issue. The vast array of entertainment we have in this country is almost mind-boggling. It also has extremely nuanced niches that are occupied from the sickest perversions to the noblest of pursuits. Yet, deciding which is which is often the subject for contentious debates. In this chapter I will try to look at both the positive and negative aspects of our society's culture. I will, in particular, try to assess how it affects the ability of our people to think and understand the world. Americans really are very individualistic compared to most nations around the world. We are also a very eclectic group of subcultures that run the gamut from the Christian right to the neo-hippies of the 21st century. Not one way of life adequately describes who we are as a nation, but I think that a current of self-determination runs through most of the groups and subsets of our society.

Until I went abroad I never realized how much of a product of our culture I really am. I am extremely religious on one hand, but completely believe that each person has to decide how they view their own personal cosmology. I am a musician and writer, yet I greatly enjoy a variety sports (though I am not good at actually playing them). I detest the debauched lowbrow humor of so many in the field of entertainment, but I am an avid fan of what others may believe to be equally base (namely *The Simpsons* and *South Park*). I appreciate the beauty of a fine woman, but often feel that our culture is overly sexualized and denigrates women with continual objectification. Ultimately, I am as eclectic as the nation is as a whole. In some ways America has so much to offer the world, yet so much of what we export in terms of popular culture drags the world down to the lowest common denominator.

One point that I would like to express before I go any further is that I am a firm believer in the marketplace of ideas. Except in the most extreme circumstances I do not believe in censorship or banning specific forms of entertainment. Regulation, on the other hand, is acceptable where it is appropriate, pornography probably being the most obvious example of such reasonable restrictions. If one does not like what one hears or sees, the simplest answer is to turn the channel or move the dial. America is founded on the freedom of choice and expression. This means that we have to tolerate what we do not feel to be edifying to our society. And in cases where people think that they need to express their opinion against some particular medium or individual, they should beware. Boycotts and protests usually only serve to draw more media attention to their intended targets and increase their effect on the culture as a whole.

We do have to understand the intense effect that images, words, slogans, and the arts can have on the mind of a nation. We are in the early stages of an explosion of technologies that did not exist for the entire history of the world prior to around 1900. The descendants of the phonograph, moving pictures, the printed media and telecommunications greatly affect the way people associate and view the world. The comprehension of how the mass media affects the psyche is only in its rudimentary stages. In one moment those who live in the developed world may take in more sensory input than people of the past would have had in an hour or even a day. We also have the benefit, and detraction, of having the experiences of life shown to us through video and audio. Before the advent of the camera one had to be in a war to endure its horrors. Today all we have to do is turn on a TV or open a magazine. For those of us who live in this society it may be hard to grasp just how much influence all of these inputs have onto how we experience the world.

I'll use an example to illustrate this point. During WWI (the first major conflict to be put onto film) the British government thought it would be a good idea to play some footage of the war in local theater houses. They chose a short film about the Battle of the Somme. This battle was one of the worst on the Western Front of the war. The British suffered particularly high casualty rates. To the amazement of the propagandists the film had an incredible effect on those who saw it. It would probably be considered mild by today's standard, but the footage caused very strong reactions to those who saw it. Troops on leave from the front went into what we would call flashbacks. Ordinary civilians, both men and women, cried out in the theaters and others became physically ill. The lesson wasn't lost on the government: for the duration of the war no battle footage was shown again to the public.

We who see the extremes of war on television, whether it is real or dramatized, are desensitized to the brutality that we are actually witnessing. Repeat this in every other aspect of society and it is no wonder that the extremes of what is acceptable are being pushed on all sides. Sexuality is beamed across the airwaves incessantly, blasphemy is spoken at the drop of a hat, and the most crude and disgusting language and behavior are always available for all to see or hear. Again, I want to stress that I do understand the subjectivity of what I am expressing. Oftentimes some of my favorite entertainments cross lines that I don't wish to be crossed. When this happens I change the channel, and when it happens enough I simply stop tuning in.

One of the biggest problems that I see with popular culture is that it has assisted in the degradation of our society as a whole. This can be particularly said of intelligence. Average citizens are fast becoming idiots. They have no knowledge of higher culture, they are ignorant of world affairs, and are essentially unable to answer the most basic questions about history and science. Too many people spend all their time in the world of make believe. I have actually had students that thought that *The Flintstones* was an accurate portrayal of the lives of cavemen. I know adults that don't know that French is spoken in Quebec. Most college graduates have a hard time finding Iraq on a map. I have had people be surprised when I referred to the sun as a star, and even go as far as to argue about it with me (though not for too long). How this ignorance has gotten to the point it has is beyond me. Yet, we must do something to increase the value we place on those pursuits that most exemplify what is great in the human race. If we don't we will only continue to spiral into this cultural sewer.

Part of the phenomenon of the dumbing down of our culture can be traced to the vast explosion of the media in the last several decades. The news is presented in short, shallow stories, politics has been reduced to sound bites, and what passes for art these days is usually little more than drivel. We have also become so couched in sarcasm that it is becoming increasingly difficult to know when someone is, or is not, being serious. The fact that a significant portion of the people who watch Jon Stewart on *The Daily Show* think that he is a legitimate source for news shows how far down we have fallen. Comedy, and I use that term loosely, is not a forum to learn about world events.

Then we have the abyss of BET, MTV, and the so-called reality shows. I purposely try to watch some of the garbage on television so that I have an informed perspective when dealing with my students and the youth culture as a whole. BET is probably more detrimental to black people than anything else on TV. It glorifies gangs, drug use, misogyny, and materialism. MTV does just about the same, but has the added motive of encouraging homosexuality. And the programs that are passed off as reality TV are the most exploitative train wrecks I have ever witnessed. The dysfunction that is portrayed as acceptable behavior is preposterous. Most of the people on these shows need to be locked up for their own good and the safety of others. Anyone who believes that this filth does not pollute the mind of our young people is naïve.

Then we have our good old friends in Hollywood. The film industry promotes perversion, incivility, anti-capitalist and anti-Western agendas, bias towards men, insincerity, anti-religious ideals, and just about all that is base in human nature. Film after film is made that denigrates the United States and implies that we are reaping what we have sown in the world. Every traditional value is ridiculed and the agenda of the left is promulgated as if it were fact. Under the guise of fantasy and artistic license we see all that has made our country great attacked. Filmmakers can do what they want, but it is rare that they ever come up with something that is original or not a piece of propaganda.

As much as I love certain sports I feel that they too are harming our culture; not so much the competitions themselves but the distraction that they have become. Too many people spend all of their time following the annals of professional sports. Many who can recite with encyclopedic accuracy the statistics from the last several decades of any given sport can barely identify who is president or what party they are from. I love my Yankees and follow them avidly, but the world does not rise or fall on their exploits (though I can be pretty caustic when they fail to win the World Series). I have no problem with those who follow professional sports except when they do it to the exclusion of all the other interests and aspects of society that are truly important to our life on this planet. Sports are an interesting pastime, but there is more to life than games.

The Internet is a new problem. In many ways it is a blessing from God, but in just as many ways it is a spawn from hell. On the one hand we have the near infinite access to information; on the other hand we have to contend with the fact that so much of that information is inaccurate or erroneous. The Internet is a forum that has little oversight. Many of these widely accepted sources for information can be distorted, or even worse. Frequency of recitation does not make for truth. This problem is exacerbated when we look to the reality that just about any image can be doctored or fabricated. Too often I have to tell my students that the information they found on the Internet is unverifiable and therefore meaningless. The problem is that the continued repetition of some of these falsehoods places them into the mindset of the overall culture.

Years ago the average person felt that he or she did not know enough facts to express an opinion. Today it is the opposite: the average person does not feel that the need to have facts to back up an opinion. This is the effect of the age of information that we live in. Popular culture has a strong influence over how we perceive ourselves as individuals. Too much of what we consume from our entertainment belittles our humanity. My only suggestion is that each of us, on our own, refrains from participating in what we feel diminishes us as people. And to those of us who produce entertainment or the arts, and I include myself in that category, let us do our best to make sure that what we do has a positive influence on our society. It would be hard to sink much lower than what we see in the realm of entertainment today, but I hazard to say that we should expect to see much worse.

EMINENT DOMAIN AND HOW YOU NO LONGER OWN YOUR PROPERTY

The Kelo vs. New London decision of the Supreme Court in 2005 essentially stripped the property rights of all American citizens. We now only own our property at the whim of the government. The federal government will no longer stop the abuses of the states or itself when it comes to the matter of seizing private property for the use of the government under the guise of eminent domain. Yes, this power exists in the Constitution, but the founding fathers would be turning over in their graves if they knew how this was being applied in the 21st century. This decision of the Supreme Court is possibly as bad as the Dred Scott case in the 1850s. The leeway that the court afforded local governments in their ability to apply this concept effectively places the property of all Americans at the mercy of petty politicians in town halls and state capitals across this nation.

Without getting too legalistic we need to look at the basic parameters which this case laid out. When reading the decision it becomes apparent that the justices essentially gave the power to any government in the United States to seize property from individuals for any reason that they deem fit. This is not the intent of eminent domain in our Constitution. We have to look to the origins of this concept to fully comprehend the error of the court. The exact phrase eminent domain does not appear in the federal Constitution. It is expressed in the last line of the Fifth Amendment, which states, "Nor shall private property be taken for public use without just compensation." Eminent domain is a concept from English common law that predates the founding of our nation. It was not intended to be used as a money machine for the government. Its purpose is to facilitate the government in times of crisis and for the use of the greater public good. Kelo broadens these ideas to the point that increasing tax revenue is reason enough for our property to be seized. The abuse of this decision is not only theoretical, but a reality as well. All over the country ordinary citizens are losing their homes, businesses, and livelihoods to the over zealous application of eminent domain.

The saving grace for this issue is the fact that the ruling on Kelo was not made when justices Roberts and Alito were on the court. Undoubtedly, both of them will see this as an unconstitutional extension of eminent domain. Yet, we have to wait for a case to present itself to the Supreme Court in order for them to have a chance to be involved in a decision on this issue. I cannot see how these sensible justices could rule in any other way than to overturn the Kelo vs. New London decision. Americans are being unjustly stripped of their property. Citizens are being persecuted by the greedy grasp of corrupt politicians. If this ruling is not overturned it would unquestionably be one in a long line of the litany of offenses that we can ascribe to our government in a new Declaration of Independence.

Right now this conception of eminent domain is being applied in only a sporadic manner, but if it were to be utilized more broadly Americans would have to take all necessary action to end its implementation. How can we build our lives in this country if the constant threat looms over one's head that at any moment everything you have worked to establish in your life can be replaced by a check from the government? Not only is this antithetical to the beliefs that this nation was founded upon, but it is an affront to the rights that we have been endowed with by our creator. Does not the Constitution state that the citizens of the United States cannot be "deprived of life, liberty, or property"? What else do they think that this form of eminent domain does except to deprive us of life, liberty, or property?

Aside from the military implementations of this concept we do have to look to its other practical uses. Roads, bridges, schools, hospitals, and other infrastructure necessities are clearly what is intended when we speak of eminent domain. Other projects and developments such as stadiums, business districts, and large-scale buildings are some of the other legitimate ways in which this concept can be applied. The World Trade Center was built on land that was claimed in just such a manner. The border fence has had some use of eminent domain in order to access the land of property owners who were unwilling to work with the federal government. We can also point toward using this government power to restore blighted neighborhoods, but we must ensure that it is not used to remove impoverished communities from cities and towns. Eminent domain has practical applications, but we must simply use common sense when preventing its abuse.

This issue is one of those issues that we should not have to even discuss. Yet, we have to due to the inherent penchant of some members of our species to be greedy. The purposes of such legal concepts are readily apparent to anyone who understands our history and culture. Problems of this nature only arise when people, who for their own selfish or misguided reasons, try to manipulate our system of government for their own gain. What astounds me is that the highest court in the land was able to deem this use of eminent domain constitutional. How could justices who should understand the basic nature of our legal system allow for such an obvious abuse of this power?

As it stands now anything that you own can be taken from you if the governing body that takes it can show how it will increase its tax revenue. This is especially true when it comes to homes and buildings used for business. Think about what this actually means in terms of its potential applications. Anyone who owns property on a stretch of highway that has come into greater use over the last several years may have their land confiscated to have it turned over to a developer who can put something in its place that will yield higher property taxes. If some construction company can build numerous condo units on the same property where you now have a single home or business it will be legal for the government to use eminent domain. When increasing tax revenue is allowed to be the basis for seizing the property of private citizens, we no longer have recourse in the courts. If the Supreme Court will not remedy the situation then it may become necessary to make a constitutional amendment that will.

If this current definition of eminent domain is not overturned by amendment or by the Supreme Court, the problems it will cause will be catastrophic. Should the time ever come that this abuse is reinforced legally by another case we will see an explosion in the confiscation of property. The unfortunate scenarios we see now will be exponentially multiplied. Once greedy politicians have this precedent validated they will find all sorts of new ways to grease their palms. We already have to watch out for the quid pro quo in our system of government today. Could you imagine what will happen if the court fails to rein in this corruption? Government officials could trade property to the highest bidder. Backroom deals could be made between unscrupulous individuals and politicians. Nothing in this country would be safe from the threat of confiscation. In short, everything you own would only be yours if those in the government allowed you to keep it. Is not tyranny living at the mercy of another?

EMBRYONIC STEM CELLS, CLONING, AND GENETIC ENGINEERING, WHEN SCIENCE BECOMES PLAYING GOD

As we enter the twenty-first century, mankind is at the threshold of many innovative scientific discoveries. In the last century we saw the development of technology on an unprecedented level in history. Never before had the human race moved so far in such a short period of time. With that development came many grave and serious moral dilemmas, some of which are still debated today. If the twentieth century presented such ethical issues, imagine what this century will bring. Some of the powers that we now possess are far beyond our capacity to control; this is especially true of genetic engineering. The natural world is not a laboratory; once we let the genie out of the bottle we may never be able to rein it back in. The laws of unintended consequences can have dire effects.

The issue of stem cells is more complex than the way in which it is usually portrayed. In most cases the liberal press tries to lump all of the varied means of securing stem cells together. This is usually done in a tone that tries to make those opposed to embryonic stem cells seem as if they are unenlightened impediments to the progress of science. It is also usually characterized as if the right is hard-hearted and unfeeling towards those facing illnesses that might find cures from stem cells. As usual, this couldn't be further from the truth. The only type of stem cell research that anyone that I know of opposes is research that uses harvested embryonic stem cells.

How one gets stem cells is one of the most contentious points in this debate. First of all, there are several types of stem cells. Each type of cell can be retrieved by using differing methods. These cells are also specific to different stages of life, pregnancy and birth. Many people are now having their babies' umbilical cord blood saved to preserve the stem cells that are in it. The problem that I, and many others, have with embryonic stem cells is the manufacturing of embryos for their use in research. The practice of harvesting embryos is a direct affront to the right to life. These embryos are created for the sole purpose of taking their stem cells. This is an egregious use of human beings. Essentially, these lives are created with the express purpose of using these cells for the potential treatment of others. There is no reason to do this when these cells can be gotten by other methods. It is also wrong to begin life with the intent of discarding it as if it were just some blob of tissue.

On top of the ethical problems with harvesting embryonic stem cells is the problem with their practical uses. Thus far, all of the achievements in this field have been made with other types of stem cells. In general, embryonic stem cells have been known to create more complications than cures. The cells have a tendency to cause tumors and have also been known to basically go haywire in the body. Stem cells are basically cells that can assume the form of specific types of cells in the body. When this process is initiated with embryonic stem cells they have a tendency get out of control. Other forms of stem cells have produced much more reliable results. Therefore it is these cells that should be first on the block for research. Embryonic cells that already exist for research and embryonic cells that are not gotten by the harvesting process should still be able to be used.

Now the greater specter of Frankenstein is to be found in cloning and genetic engineering. I will deal with cloning first. Many know of the cloned sheep Dolly, which was created in Britain. What many do not know is the complications that she underwent during her life. This poor sheep was not the miracle that her creators claimed her to be. In fact, if anything Dolly only proved the inadequacy of man when we try to play God. Dolly was subject to frequent sickness, poor functioning, and advanced aging. She led a sad life and died very young. This same process has been repeated in other animals that scientists have tried to clone.

We also have to look at the ethical and scientific dilemmas posed by cloning. If we were to ever gain control over this process we would have to beware of the considerable dangers involved. First we have the possibility that some of the inadequacies faced by Dolly may be inherent in the proteins contained in the bodies of animals that we clone. We do not know how to quantify such a possibility and it may be a much more significant problem than we yet realize. The potential for a buildup of specific proteins endemic to any line of cloned animals may be catastrophic over the long haul. What this means in simple terms is that the use of the same genes to mass produce animals, and even plants, may harbor some material that if it were consumed repeatedly may build up and become a poison or carcinogen over time. Just because mankind can do something doesn't necessarily mean that we should. Cloning sounds innocuous to some, but I believe that it is fraught with dangers that we don't even know exist at this point. Furthermore, it is imperative that we consider what will happen when these cloned animals and plants make their way into the natural environment. Almost every species we have domesticated has a feral population that now exists in the wild. Cloned animals may be susceptible to problems in life, but if we were to release a creature with a specific gene that favors these clones over a natural population, they could cause related species to become extinct. This is already occurring worldwide with the introduction of foreign species into local eco-systems with catastrophic results.

The most frightening of all prospects on the man-playing-God stage is genetic engineering. The dangers that are posed by this misuse of science are truly terrifying. We have learned how to specifically manipulate genes in various plants and animals. This is not only done on a species by species basis, but scientists have crossed the genes of different species at times. This has been done using animal genes in plants and vice-versa. The potential for apocalyptic scenarios with genetic engineering is not fiction, but a reality. This is an area that mankind should seriously reconsider fooling around with. The unintended consequences that could result from our further pursuit of this science are incalculable. Each gene is a treasure trove of information. They all have encoded within them the information for numerous purposes. They also have a vast amount of hidden information which we have only begun to grasp. The uncertainties that lie at the heart of genetic engineering are myriad and beyond our ability to comprehend. Much like the dangers that nuclear waste pose, these genetic unknowns could have the potential to infiltrate every corner of the biological earth. Once these plagues are unleashed into the world we will never be able to contain them. This alone makes me turn away in disgust at the very thought of genetic engineering.

Let us look at one case in point. A specific breed of corn was genetically engineered to produce its own insecticide. In fact, it worked quite well. In fact, it worked too well. The insecticide produced by the corn was so effective that it killed any monarch butterflies that crossed into the area where they were planted. The butterflies are already facing a number of problems that threaten their species. So many butterflies were killed by this genetically engineered corn that their population was significantly reduced. What will happen when we have far more potent unintended consequences from our manipulation of the genetic code that exists within the DNA of all living creatures?

One of the greatest dangers that genetic engineering poses is the ability to infect the genes of natural species. Genetically engineered plants and animals are already starting to be used around the world. Currently the European Union is much more hostile towards these agricultural experiments than the U.S. government. This is one of the few cases where I find myself more in agreement with the EU than I do my own government. In the United States, genetic engineering experiments are being conducted in universities and by companies in agri-business. The potential for these manipulated species to enter the gene pools of the natural eco-systems is virtually inevitable. Once the natural individuals are infected with these man altered genes the process is out of our hands. We already have significant problems dealing with invader species; how much less will we have the power to contend with genetically altered wildlife?

I believe one of the most dangerous possibilities that exist from genetic engineering would be the creation of a warm-blooded creature that reproduced rapidly. This would be especially true of a species that reproduced by spores, like a fungus, but maintained the voracious appetite of warm-blooded animals. If we think rats and mice are pests, this would make them look like a mere annoyance. This is why we have to resist the temptation to cross the lines of the kingdoms of life. Taking genes from one kingdom to another will have results that there is no way for us to foretell. We barely understand the genetic code as it exists in any one species, no matter how simple they may be. How do we think that we can predict the effects from us crossing genes from one species to another?

Aside from all the apocalyptic scenarios, I have to admit there is one area where I find myself drawn to when it comes to genetic engineering, and that is the possibility of reproducing extinct species. At once when it comes to this subject I find myself dreaming of a living breathing Tyrannosaurus Rex or wooly mammoth and the deepest pangs of my soul, which tell me these are endeavors better left to the pens of science fiction writers. Species have become extinct for a reason and mankind needs to leave it that way. We have no idea what the results would be from such experiments. The possibility of unleashing a pandemic pathogen is probably the most dangerous effect that we would yield from playing God in this realm. As bad and predictable as the movies of the *Jurassic Park series* are, the lesson they impart is elementary. If God wants us to find dinosaurs then they will still be hidden in the remote jungles of the world or the depths of the oceans.

The human race has already unleashed the power of the atom. The bombings of Hiroshima and Nagasaki have shown us the horrific affects that come with what we now have at our fingertips. The dangers of radioactive waste also indicate the inability of mankind to deal with the products of our technology. How much more potential for disaster does the prospect of playing God with the biologic world pose? We are not simply talking about using what God has put in place, like when we use the existing genes to produce hybrids; we are talking about fundamentally altering the genetic basis for species and even at times mixing them together. This is no longer science, but the work of madmen. We need to remember that we are not omnipotent, but fallible and imperfect human beings. The products of our efforts can reach far beyond what we ever intended. Therefore, we need to refrain from experiments that permit for our manipulations to become part of the natural world. There is science and then there is Frankenstein. Let us realize which is which.

WHY WE NEED GUANTANAMO

If it weren't for the liberals we wouldn't need Guantanamo. If it weren't for the ACLU, leftist judges, and anti-war activists we would not have to hold those captured on the battlefield in military facilities beyond our borders and beyond our courts. It is their twisting of the legal system and the traditional prosecution of war that has forced our government to create a place like Guantanamo. If we were allowed to maintain the common sense approach that we followed in past wars we could safely hold these enemy combatants on military bases on our own soil, but the liberals have gone off the deep end in their attempts to create rights for those prisoners of war we are holding. They have not only abrogated the Constitution, but the Geneva Conventions as well. The terrorists we are fighting do not meet any of the criteria that would qualify them as legal combatants.

Before we go into any of the legal and moral arguments about Guantanamo we first need to look at the practical debate. How many of the prisoners released from Guantanamo have been recaptured on the battlefields again? Why should we release any prisoner unless it has been proven that they have been wrongly accused? How in the world did the left ever arrive at the idea that enemy combatants have the right to a trial by jury in our court system? To me all of these questions point in one obvious direction. The liberals have no comprehension of what war is and how it has been traditionally fought. They also do not realize how the asymmetric warfare utilized by our enemies has changed the way in which we need to treat the prisoners we capture on the battlefield.

The enemy we fight wears no uniform. The enemy we fight is not part of the military of any nation. The enemy we fight hides among the civilian population. The enemy we fight has no established command structure. The enemy we fight uses the local people as shields for their operations and attacks. The enemy we fight has no limit to their methods of warfare. The enemy we fight has made the entire planet their frontline. The enemy we fight is comprised of terrorists, not legal combatants. This enemy does not constitute a military as it is traditionally defined. Therefore the only obligation we have is to treat them humanely, and even that is being generous. Never before in history have we granted constitutional rights to legal combatants, so why should we grant them to terrorists?

In the past we have used military tribunals to try prisoners of war. This should be sufficient for us in this conflict. Yet, it is the radical left that has attempted to confer rights to the prisoners of this war that we have never given to prisoners of any war. Anyone of those we hold has the ability to take their case before the military. Why should any further leeway be given to those we have captured? They have the recourse that is necessary if they want to prove that they have been erroneously imprisoned. Several people held in Guantanamo have already been released under just these circumstances. No one is trying to imprison innocent people.

If the liberals were to ever get trials for these prisoners in open court it would be a disaster. The damage done to our ability to prosecute this war would be irreparable. We cannot have the government, military, and intelligence agencies revealing their methods for capturing the terrorists in open court. Not only will this reveal our tactics, but it will endanger our troops and our allies in the countries we are fighting. In every war there are secrets, why should this war be any different? When these combatants are American citizens, such as Jose Padilla, then the circumstance is different, but even here some attention needs to be given to the sensitive interests of national security. The court system is not a place for terrorists to be tried.

Traditionally prisoners of war have been paroled, exchanged, or held for the duration of the war. Spies, on the other hand, were executed often without trial. Even when they were tried it was before a military tribunal not the civilian courts. British Major John Andre, associate of Benedict Arnold, was captured by American forces during our revolution without a uniform and with the plans for West Point on his person. None other than George Washington had him hanged as a spy. During WWII, a number of German spies were caught in New York City and Chicago; they were tried by a military commission and all but two were executed. If this is the traditional methods of dealing with prisoners of war and spies, why should we change the way we operate when we are fighting one of the most inhumane enemies that we have ever fought?

It is the fault of the Jihadists that they have declared an indefinite war. Since there is no limit to their fight and no limit to their battlefield we have to hold them as prisoners for as long as it takes. Their indefinite detention is the result of their actions. Guantanamo has become a necessity because we have no alternative to keeping these enemies off the battlefield. For those who claim that they have been wrongly imprisoned the military has mechanisms by which they can prove their case.

Many in this country are worried about the stature of America in the international community. They worry about our image on the world stage. Frankly I could give a damn about what the world thinks of us when we are doing what is necessary for our national defense. Most European nations have lost all will to fight. They try to use diplomacy to solve every problem, and when that doesn't work their answer is more diplomacy or toothless sanctions. If they hate Guantanamo so much, why don't they offer an alternative solution? Instead we have to listen to the complaints of Amnesty International, spitting out ludicrous comparisons of the U.S. to truly tyrannical regimes. We need to do what is in our best interest. The international community can love us or hate us, but we should never bow to their supposed wisdom. Wasn't it Neville Chamberlain who prevented WWII by going to Munich and forging an agreement with Hitler and Mussolini? Oh, right, that didn't work out so well.

We also have to contend with the ridiculous claims that we are torturing the prisoners at Guantanamo. If this was true why have so many of the prisoners refused repatriation to their home countries? Is it possible that they fear real torture at the hands of their home nation's government? Being locked in a cold room with loud music does not constitute torture. Being given three meals a day, a place to sleep, a yard to play soccer in, and having the ability to practice a form of religion that you use to hate us is not torture. Whenever there have been real reports of maltreatment, like Abu Ghraib, we have moved to quickly remedy the situation. The liberals have to stop equating the U.S. with people like the Nazis. It not only is absurd, but it diminishes the real suffering that people have endured in the past and are enduring as I write in places like North Korea.

If we did not have to worry about the radical left conferring rights on these enemy combatants that they don't have, we could house these prisoners here. Yet, we know that the courts will eventually hear these cases if we did, and the enemy will score another victory. Then we'll have to start sending lawyers out onto the battlefield with our troops to discuss if their every action was legal and had the approval of the international community. How did it ever come to this? How come so many Americans, and Westerners as a whole, have formed these notions about playing nice in war? I'm against torture, I'm against unnecessary brutality toward our enemy, I also don't want to falsely imprison someone, but we cannot win this war if we don't treat the enemy as an enemy. Guantanamo is not the problem; it is the liberals who want to give civilian trials to terrorists and illegal combatants that is.

LIBERAL VS. CONSERVATIVE: A CONCLUSION

Our nation and world will be faced with innumerable challenges over the course of the next several decades. Some of those challenges are domestic in nature and others affect the international community as a whole. The United States of America is the greatest nation on earth. We are an integral part of the society of humans across the globe. What we do, or do not do, as a country will certainly help determine the paths that mankind takes in addressing the problems of the 21st century. We now stand at the crossroads of a great divide in human history we can either follow the way of the liberal or the way of the conservative. The difference between these two ideologies could be the difference between a society that survives and a society that falls into a new dark age.

Over the course of this book I have tried to show the disparate ways in which the liberals and conservatives try to address the issues that confront the human race. In some cases they are mere differences of policy and preference; in others they are a battle of the quintessential ideals of what it is to be human. Many of the disagreements between the left and the right are no longer simple matters of differing viewpoints, but they are examples of a fundamental divide about the nature and purpose of society itself. We are fast coming to a point that the methods with which we govern our day-to-day lives will not be acceptable to those who hold to either of these two philosophies. One of the two ideologies will have to ascend to the reins of power and when one does, those who are of the other may find the culture they are forced to live in is unacceptable. This is when we may face civil war.

When I first entered into college I thought of myself as a moderate who leaned toward the left. On many issues I disagreed with the established liberals, such as the right to life, but in general I thought that I held to values that they espoused. Then while rummaging through a box of books being offered for sale in the William Paterson College student center, I came across a book called *On Conservatism*. Originally I bought the book with the purpose of knowing the mind of my enemy, but as I began to read the book I came to realize that in actuality I was a conservative. One of the main themes in the book was the idea of an organic society. This concept truly exemplified the way in which I viewed the world. It was best explained by juxtaposing the French and American revolutions. It was pointed out that the American Revolution was a conservative revolution, whereas the French Revolution was a liberal revolution. The Americans merely tried to trim the tree of society, but the French cut the whole thing down. We tried to establish a nation based on long-held concepts of the rights of man, whereas the French tried to create a whole new basis for society. America produced the Declaration of Independence, but the French gave us metric time and even a metric calendar. In America there was some social upheaval, but nothing compared to the bloody class warfare that was witnessed in France. History has shown which of the two ideologics is the more powerful and stable.

I feel that one of the greatest failings in the American conservative movement is the ignorance on issues of the environment. I understand the hostility towards the loony environmentalist whackos, but anyone who pays any attention to nature must understand that our society is having a very negative impact on the eco-systems of our planet. As I said in my chapter on the environment, the root word in conservative is conserve. The natural resources of this planet are finite and very delicately balanced. In order to best utilize them for our own needs, and the preservation of the world that God has given us, we must learn to maintain our environment in far more conservative manners. Six-and-a-half billion of any species of our size could have an extensive impact on their environment. Couple that with our technological power and it becomes evident that we need to monitor the effects that we have on our Earth.

I feel that one of the most discerning differences between the liberals and conservatives is our views on the sanctity of life. For the most part the liberals take the position that we are but mere biological creatures. Conservatives, on the other hand, tend to believe that we are products of the God that created us. It is hard to ascertain exactly how many issues that these differing points of view actually affect, but it is a significant divide on how we view the world and society as a whole. The difference between believing life is a mere amalgamation of molecules or divinely created is incalculable. This distinction is probably one of the biggest differences between the truly conservative and the truly liberal. We see it every day in the ways in which people carry out their lives. If we are purely biological then the entire way we live life is based on a different foundation than if we believe that we were created by a divine being. Obviously, I am not proposing that all on the left do not believe in God, but that by and large their ideals are founded on or viewed through a secular lens.

One of the more significant disparities that the conservatives and liberals have is our ideas on the purpose of government. The left seems to believe that the government should be used as a tool to shape society and socially engineer our culture. They feel that we need to use the government to ensure that the amenities of life are guaranteed to all. The right tends toward the ideal that the government should play a limited role in the society. The conservatives think, as Ronald Regan said, "The government that governs best governs least." These two ideas are not always mutually exclusive, but we see this divide quite prominently in this presidential election. The Democrats will turn this country into a socialist state if they win the presidency and maintain their majority in Congress. Yes, the government should be used at times to assist those in need in this nation, but we must be careful that it does not grow into an insatiable monster. The federal government is already too expensive, too invasive, and far too expansive. We need less government, not more!

The current crop of liberals likes to be against things. The only things that they seem to be for are raising taxes, killing babies, and surrendering to terrorists. They constantly harp about the war in Iraq, yet never offer any viable alternatives. They refuse to suggest anything other than diplomacy and working with our allies on any foreign policy issues, despite the fact that this has failed time and time again. I would love to live in a world without enemies, but this is not the reality that we face. The liberals either refuse to accept this or are just completely naïve. If we follow the policies that they will bring to the White House, the enemies we face today will be infinitely stronger when we have to face them in the future anyway. Strength now will mean less war in the years to come.

As much of a disaster that the liberals would be on the world stage they will be equally devastating on the domestic front. They will wreck our economy with higher taxes and unnecessary regulations. Their raising of the capital gains tax would be a virtual assault on the stock market. Their continued influence in the public school system would ensure its continued spiral down. The amnesty that they would offer to illegal aliens will create tens of millions of new citizens, most of whom are poorly educated and unskilled. In short, their atheistic, agnostic secularism would further seep into every corner of society. That which is evil will be considered good and that which is good will be considered evil. I think I might have heard that somewhere before. I wonder where?

All one needs to do to assess the disaster that will befall us if the liberals gain any more power is to look at the nations of western

Europe. They are economic basket cases that are overburdened by their socialist healthcare and retirement systems. On foreign policy they are effete and loquacious windbags who never saw an enemy to which they wouldn't surrender. In the name of humanism they have embraced every perversion and social sickness known to mankind. Their secularism has led them to restrict free speech and curtail freedom of religion. And they have raised a generation that is almost completely devoid of the concept of God. If you find these ideals appealing, then all you need to do is vote for more leftist candidates; if you don't then we need to take this country back in the right direction.

My intention in this book is not to be divisive, but if stating my opinions has that effect then so be it. This is a crucial time in the history of this nation and the world. We can't afford to circumvent the debates we need to have with polite words and sensitivity towards feelings. I have done my best to address as many of the issues of our time as I could. In some places, I have been tempted to add to my statements, but I feel that what I have written about should suffice for now. It is impossible to tackle every problem in society in its totality. Hopefully I have been able to deal with them in a manner that will best exemplify the differences that exist between the liberal and the conservative points of view.

I sincerely believe in freedom. I believe that every man is given his rights by the one who created us. As much as the liberals would probably agree to these general points their policies suggest otherwise. It is they who are trying to impose their will onto the culture and society as a whole. It is they who have steadily used the government to infringe on the traditions that have made this nation great. It is they who are attempting to form a new America based on a new set of values. Yet, if it is the will of the people to create this new society then they should do so. Just don't ask me to be a willing part of this crime. I intend to stand on the principles in which I firmly believe. I will also exert every effort that God affords me to educate the people of this world to the ideals that are at the core of a good and functioning society. We need to be alert to the fact that there is an ideological war being waged on this planet and it is being fought in every area of our culture. Eventually, the day may come when this war moves from the realm of the mind onto the battlefields of actual combat. I hope that time never comes, but we must find ways in which we can live together in order to avoid that most unfortunate consequence.

Conservatism is based on the concepts of freedom, self-determination, and the sanctity of life. Conservatism tries to assess the world through the realities that exist and hopes to act utilizing the ideals that we hold dear. Society has grown into what it is over the course of time for a reason. We need to address the problems that we face in pragmatic and practical methods. Capitalism, democracy, and a strong faith in God have enabled us to become the greatest nation on earth. We must remember what it is that has allowed us to become so prosperous materially and in terms of liberty. Never before in the history of the world has one nation been so blessed by God.

2001331

Made in the USA